The First Crusade

When Pope Urban II rose to his feet to address the multitudes gathered before him at the Council of Clermont in 1095, his appeal was simple: let Western Christendom march to the aid of their brethren in the East. Whether the Crusades are regarded as the most tremendous and romantic of Christian expeditions or the last of the barbarian invasions, they remain one of the most exciting and colorful adventure stories in history. The reasons for joining the Crusade varied widely – remittance from penance, a desire to see the Holy Places, greed for the power and booty that might be captured. But the prize at the end of it all, be it spiritual or temporal, was the Holy City of Jerusalem. The journey's spectacular culmination was the long siege of Jerusalem, at the end of which the Crusaders, by a brilliant tactical maneuver, broke down its defenses and poured into the city, which erupted in a bloody massacre. Steven Runicman's *History of the Crusades* is justly acclaimed as the most complete and fascinating account of the historic journey to save the Holy Land from the infidel. This abridgment makes accessible to a wider readership one of the most compelling historical narratives.

"This is one of history's most extraordinary episodes made extraordinarily real. Written by an expert blessed with lucidity and style . . . a story that has everything." – *The Church Times*

"It reads magnificently. As an example of sustained and intelligent narrative it could hardly be bettered. Sir Steven's great achievement was to make a complicated subject appear simple and then to write it up beautifully. . . . No one is likely to surpass Sir Steven's powers of synthesis or the masterly way he writes." – *History Today*

Sir Steven Runciman (1903–2000) was the pre-eminent historian of the Crusades and the Byzantine Empire. His acclaimed *History of the Crusades* was first published from 1951 to 1954.

The First Crusade

Steven Runciman

CAMBRIDGE
UNIVERSITY PRESS

CAMBRIDGE UNIVERSITY PRESS
Cambridge, New York, Melbourne, Madrid, Cape Town, Singapore, São Paulo

Cambridge University Press
40 West 20th Street, New York, NY 10011-4211, USA

www.cambridge.org
Information on this title: www.cambridge.org/9780521847391

Original edition © Cambridge University Press 1951
First abridged edition © Cambridge University Press 1980
© Cambridge University Press 2005

First published as Volume I of *The History of the Crusades* 1951
Abridged edition first published 1980
This edition published 2005
Reprinted 2005

Printed in the United States of America

A catalog record for this publication is available from the British Library.

Library of Congress Cataloging in Publication Data

Runciman, Steven, Sir, 1903–2000
The First Crusade / Steven Runciman.
p. cm.
ISBN 0-521-84739-7 (hb) – ISBN 0-521-61148-2 (pbk.)
1. Crusades – First, 1096–1099.
D161.2.R862 1992
Dewey Class No.: 940.1/8 20

ISBN-13 978-0-521-84739-1 hardback
ISBN-10 0-521-84739-7 hardback

ISBN-13 978-0-521-61148-0 paperback
ISBN-10 0-521-61148-2 paperback

Contents

Introductory note

This work is based on the first of my three-volume *History of the Crusades*, originally published in 1951. I have abridged the introductory chapters and brought the book to a close with the Crusaders' capture of Jerusalem, so as to concentrate on the extraordinary story of the First Crusade.

The book is published without reference notes or a bibliography. If readers wish to consult the sources, primary and secondary, on which my account is based, may I refer them to the original work, in which a full *apparatus criticus* is provided? A recent edition is still in print.

S.R.

CHAPTER I

The reign of Antichrist

When ye shall see the abomination of desolation, spoken
of by Daniel the prophet, stand in the holy place.

St Matthew XXIV, 15

On a February day in the year AD 638 the Caliph Omar
entered Jerusalem, riding upon a white camel. He was dressed
in worn, filthy robes, and the army that followed him was
rough and unkempt; but its discipline was perfect. At his side
was the Patriarch Sophronius, as the chief magistrate of the
surrendered city. Omar rode straight to the site of the Temple
of Solomon, whence his friend Mahomet had ascended into
heaven. Watching him stand there, the Patriarch remembered
the words of Christ and murmured through his tears: 'Behold
the abomination of desolation, spoken of by Daniel the
prophet.'

Next, the Caliph asked to see the shrines of the Christians.
The Patriarch took him to the Church of the Holy Sepulchre
and showed him all that was there. While they were in the
church the hour for Moslem prayer approached. The Caliph
asked where he could spread out his prayer-rug. Sophronius
begged him to stay where he was; but Omar went outside to the
porch of the Martyrium, for fear, he said, lest his zealous
followers might claim for Islam the place wherein he had
prayed. And so indeed it was. The porch was taken over by the
Moslems, but the church remained as it had been, the holiest
sanctuary of Christendom.

This was according to the terms of the city's surrender. The
Prophet himself had ordained that, while the heathen should

be offered the choice of conversion or death, the People of the
Book, the Christians and the Jews, to whom by courtesy were
added the Zoroastrians, should be allowed to retain their places
of worship and to use them without hindrance; but they might
not add to them, nor might they carry arms nor ride on
horseback, and they must pay a special capitation tax, known
as the *jizya*. Sophronius could not have hoped for better terms
when he rode out on his ass under safe conduct to meet the
Caliph on the Mount of Olives, refusing to hand over his city
to anyone of lesser authority. Jerusalem with its great walls,
recently repaired, had held out for over a year against the
Moslems. But, within the city, supplies were running out; and
there was no longer any hope of relief. The countryside was in
the Caliph's hands, and one by one the cities of Syria and
Palestine had fallen to his armies. There were no Christian
troops left nearer than Egypt, except for a small garrison
holding out in Caesarea, on the coast. All that Sophronius
could obtain from the conqueror beyond the usual terms was
that Christian officials in the city might retire with their
families and their portable goods to the coast at Caesarea.

This was the Patriarch's last public achievement, the tragic
climax to a long life spent in labour for the orthodoxy and unity
of Christendom. He had preached and worked in vain. The
Arab conquest was proof of his failure. A few weeks later he
died of a broken heart.

Indeed, no human agency could have stopped the disruptive
movements in the eastern provinces of the old Roman Empire.
Throughout the Empire's history there had been a latent
struggle between East and West. The West had won politically
at Actium. But the East, Egypt and Syria in particular,
remained the richest and most populous part of the Empire.
The eastern provinces contained the main centres of industry.
Their ships and caravans controlled the trade with the Orient.
Their culture, both material and spiritual, was far higher than
that of the West. The influence of the East grew steadily
stronger, till at last the Emperor Constantine the Great
adopted an eastern religion and moved his capital eastward, to
Byzantium on the Bosphorus.

During the following century barbarian invaders took over the western provinces of the Empire. By the end of the fifth century there were barbarian kingdoms established in Gaul, in Spain, in Britain, in North Africa and finally even in Italy. In these new kingdoms, with the former Roman civil administration in ruins, it was the Roman Church that alone could provide schoolmasters and lawyers, accountants and scribes. The rulers, some heretic and some heathen, were obliged to use clerics in order to maintain a Government. The Church represented both tradition and unity; and, in the Dark Ages that followed, it succeeded, precariously at times, to preserve its unity under the authority of a single head, the Bishop of Rome.

The story was very different in the eastern provinces. They had survived the invasions mainly owing to the superb strategic situation and the formidable fortifications of the new capital. But in Syria and in Egypt the rule of Constantinople was even less popular than the rule of Rome had been. The great metropolitan centres of Antioch and Alexandria resented the upstart city whose size and wealth was beginning to surpass their own. Owing to movements far beyond the frontier, trade from the Far East was beginning to forsake the route across the Indian Ocean to the Red Sea or the Persian Gulf and to take a more northerly route that led to Constantinople, while the barbarian invasions had disrupted the trade on to the West. Worst of all, the Emperors seemed to be determined to reconquer the western provinces and to make the eastern provinces pay for their wars. In the sixth century Justinian succeeded in recovering North Africa and Italy, but only after a long struggle; and the cost in taxes fell upon his eastern subjects. Moreover, just across the Armenian mountains and the Syrian desert was the aggressive kingdom of Sassanid Persia, against whose raids the imperial forces provided inadequate protection.

In the East politics and religion have always been inter-mixed; and, in that age of faith, political discontent was expressed by religious dissent. While the Christians in the West were almost all ready to accept the doctrines put forward by the Roman See, the ancient Churches of the East tended to develop each its own theological viewpoint and its own liturgical usages. The differences were enhanced by the rivalries of the great hierarchs, headed by the Patriarchs of Alexandria and Antioch, each of them regarding himself as the equal of the Bishop of Rome and superior to the newly elevated Patriarchs of Constantinople and Jerusalem. The congregations, to whom theological niceties were a matter of intense and passionate interest, tended to follow their leaders. The doctrinal disputes centred round the problem of the true nature of Christ. The Emperors tried to preserve uniformity by summoning Oecumenical Councils, Councils to which all the bishops of Christendom were invited, in the hope that the Holy Ghost would descend on them as it had on the disciples at Pentecost. The Councils achieved unanimity only because dissident bishops either refused to vote or were prevented from voting. After each Council a section of Christendom broke away from the main body. The Arian heretics who seceded in the fourth century faded out in the East. But after the Council of Ephesus in 431 there was a separated Nestorian Church, which soon found refuge in the Zoroastrian kingdom of Persia, where it was tolerated and from which its missionaries were to travel into India and into Tartary. The Council of Chalcedon in 451 was repudiated by the far larger congregations of Monophysites in Egypt and in Syria. They did not secede at once; but attempts to conciliate them failed. By the end of the sixth century the vast majority of Egyptians belonged to the separated Coptic Church and most of the Syrians to the Church usually known as Jacobite, after its organizer, Jacob Baradaeus. The Emperors' many attempts at reconciliation came to nothing, chiefly because their Western policy made them unwilling to break with Rome. The Roman divines disliked doctrinal subtleties and would not condone any delicate formula that might serve as a compromise.

Meanwhile, by forcing civil disabilities on them, the Imperial government had alienated the many colonies of Jews scattered throughout the Empire.

In 610 the Persian king Chosroes II declared war on the Empire, which for eight years had been ruled by a savage and incompetent usurper, Phocas. Phocas had just been replaced by a young general of Armenian origin, Heraclius; but he had inherited a disorganized army and an empty treasury. When the Persians invaded Syria the Emperor's forces received no help from the local population. The invaders occupied Antioch in 611 and Damascus in 613. Only at Jerusalem, a centre of Orthodoxy, did they meet with opposition; but, with the help of the Jews within the walls, the holy city was stormed in April 614. There followed a terrible massacre of Christians; and the holiest relics of Christendom, the instruments of the Passion and the True Cross itself, were carried off to the Persian capital at Ctesiphon. During the next few years the Persians occupied Egypt, again meeting with no opposition from the populace, and their armies marched across Anatolia to join with Avar barbarians from the Steppes in a siege of Constantinople.

The fall of Jerusalem and the loss of the Cross had given a terrible shock to Christendom. The war against the Persians assumed the nature of a holy war. When Heraclius was able in 622 to take the offensive he solemnly dedicated himself and his army to God and set out as a Christian warrior fighting against the powers of darkness. To subsequent generations he figured as the first of the Crusaders. William of Tyre, writing his History of the Crusades five centuries later, included the story of the Persian war; and the old French translation of his book was entitled *L'Estoire de Eracles*.

After many moments of anxiety the Crusade was successful. The Persians were decisively defeated at Nineveh in December 627. In 629 peace was established. In August that year Heraclius celebrated his triumph in Constantinople. The following spring he travelled south to receive back the Holy Cross and to carry it in pomp to Jerusalem.

It was a moving ceremony. But when the enthusiasm had died down, Syria and Egypt were no happier than before. The Empire had been impoverished by the war; and Heraclius had only been able to finance it by a great loan from the Orthodox Church. Now the heretic Churches in Syria and Egypt found themselves once again obliged to pay high taxes, and they saw their money go straight into the coffers of the Orthodox hierarchy. Under Persian rule they had not fared badly. Their loyalty to the Christian Emperor wore thin. Like many of his predecessors, Heraclius attempted to evolve a religious compromise that would reconcile the separated Churches. But the Monoergism and the Monotheletism that he proposed satisfied nobody; and an ill-timed persecution alienated the Jews.

When Heraclius was in Constantinople in 629, receiving congratulatory embassies from as far afield as France and India, a letter is said to have arrived written to him by an Arabian chieftain who announced himself as the Prophet of God and bade the Emperor join his faith. Similar letters were sent to the Kings of Persia and Ethiopia and to the Governor of Egypt. The story is probably apocryphal. It is unlikely that Heraclius had any idea as yet of the events that were revolutionizing the Arabian peninsula. At the beginning of the seventh century Arabia was occupied by a number of unruly independent tribes, some pastoral and nomadic, some agricultural, and a few dwelling in the merchant-cities that lay along the caravan routes. They were idolaters, each district having its special idol, of which the most revered was the *kaabah* at Mecca, the richest of the merchant-cities; but there was an old tradition of monotheism, known as the *hanif*. Jewish, Zoroastrian and Christian missionaries were working in the peninsula, the most successful being the Monophysite Christians, who had converted some of the tribes on the fringe of the desert and who had churches all along the caravan routes. At the same time the slender resources of the peninsula, grown slenderer since the destruction of the irrigation works of the old Himyarite kingdom, were insufficient for the increasing population. Throughout recorded history the desert peoples had constantly overflowed into the cultivated lands around. Now the pressure was particularly strong.

The peculiar and tremendous genius of Mahomet was exactly suited to these circumstances. He came from Mecca, a poor relation of its great clan, the Qoraishites. He had travelled and seen something of the world and its religions. He was attracted by Monophysite Christianity; but the doctrine of the Trinity seemed to him inconsistent with the monotheism of the *hanif* tradition, which he admired. The doctrine that he evolved did not reject Judaism or Christianity but was put forward as a newer revelation which simplified and purified the faith. His success as a religious leader was mainly due to his complete understanding of his fellow Arabs. At the same time, he possessed extraordinary political skill. In ten years he was able to build up out of nothing an empire that was poised to conquer the world. In 622, the year of the Hegira, when he was forced to flee from Mecca to Medina, his only following was his household and a small group of friends. In 632, when he died, he was lord of Arabia, and his armies were crossing its frontiers. In the East adventurers often rise and fall. But Mahomet left an organization whose permanence was guaranteed by the Koran. This remarkable work, compiled by the Prophet as the Word of God, contains not only uplifting maxims and stories but also rules for the conduct of life and a complete code of laws for the governance of an empire. It was simple enough to be accepted by his Arab contemporaries and universal enough to suit the needs of the vast dominion that his successors were to build. Indeed the strength of his faith, Islam, lay in its simplicity. There was one God in Heaven, one Commander of the Faithful to rule on earth, and one law, the Koran, by which he should rule. Unlike Christianity, which preached a peace never achieved, Islam unashamedly came with a sword.

The sword struck at the Roman Empire even during the Prophet's life-time, with small raids into Palestine. Under his successor, Abu Bakr, the raids grew fiercer, and an Arab army reached the Mediterranean coast at Gaza. Under Omar, who became Caliph in 634, the raids became wars of conquest; and Heraclius, who was in northern Syria, had to take action. But his treasury was empty and his troops exhausted; and the local population would give him no support. He sent his brother Theodore with the local Syrian troops to restore order in Palestine; but Theodore was decisively beaten by the Arabs at Ajnadain, south of Jerusalem. Soon afterwards the Caliph captured Damascus and Homs. Heraclius was seriously alarmed; but the army that he scraped together was routed on the banks of the river Yarmuk, southeast of the Sea of Galilee, when the Christian Arabs serving with the army deserted to the enemy. They were Monophysites who hated the Emperor; and their pay was long overdue.

Heraclius was at Antioch when the news of the battle reached him. He could do no more. After a service of intercession in Antioch cathedral, he went to the coast and took ship to Constantinople, crying as he left the shore: 'Farewell, a long farewell to Syria.'

The Arabs quickly overran the country. The Christian population submitted to them without demur; and the Jews gave them active help. Only at Jerusalem and Caesarea was there any organized resistance. But there was little hope. The Patriarch Sophronius hastily repaired the defences of his city; but he carefully sent all the holy Christian relics, with the exception of part of the True Cross, for safety to Constantinople. Antioch fell to the Caliph in 638, the same year as Jerusalem. Caesarea held out to 639.

In the meantime Persia, which was more exhausted even than the Roman Empire after the long war, had fallen into the Caliph's hands. A victory at Kadesiah in 637 gave the Arabs control of Iraq, and a second victory the following year at Nekhavend gave them the Iranian plateau. During the next few years their armies reached the Oxus valley and the mountains of Afghanistan.

In December 639, an Arab army entered Egypt. Babylon (Old Cairo) fell in 640, and the great city of Alexandria in 642. It was recaptured by the Christians for a time in 643, then lost for ever. By the year 700 the Arabs had overrun all the coastlands of North Africa. Eleven years later they occupied Spain. By 717 their empire stretched from the Pyrenees to central India and their warriors were hammering at the gates of Constantinople.

This marked the limit of Arab expansion. Arab armies crossed the Pyrenees but were driven back; and they failed to capture Constantinople, retiring back behind the Taurus mountains and leaving Anatolia in Christian hands. Fighting along the frontiers became a series of raids rather than wars of conquest. But there seemed little chance that the Roman

Empire, Byzantium, as it now might be called, would rise again to rescue the Holy Places. The Christians of the East had to accept the rule of infidel masters.

Many of them were happy to do so. Unlike the Christian Empire, which had tried to enforce religious uniformity on its citizens, the Caliphate was prepared to accept religious minorities, provided that they were People of the Book. The Christians, with the Zoroastrians and the Jews, became *dhimmis*, or protected peoples, free to worship as they pleased so long as they paid the *jizya*, a capitation tax later transformed into a tax paid in lieu of military service, and a land tax, the *kharaj*. Each sect was treated as a *milet*, a semi-autonomous community within the state, each under its religious leader who was responsible for its good behaviour. Each was to keep those places of worship that it had possessed at the time of the conquest: though in fact several churches were taken over and others destroyed by the Moslems. New religious buildings could be erected so long as they were no taller than Moslem buildings and the sounds of their bells and services were inaudible to Moslem ears. But the *dhimmis* had to wear distinctive clothes, and they might not ride on horseback nor bear arms; nor should they ever offend against Moslem practices nor attempt to convert Moslems nor marry Moslem women; and they must remain loyal to the state.

The system favoured the Orthodox Christian communities, who called themselves the Melkites, the Emperor's men, and the Moslem authorities recognized that the Emperor had the right to be interested in their welfare. The heretic churches had no such lay protector. Many of their adherents drifted over to Islam, to enjoy the advantages of belonging to the ruling community. Within a century of the conquest Syria and Palestine were predominantly Moslem countries. The growth of Islam was not due to a sudden influx of Arabs from the desert. The pure Arabs formed little more than a military caste. The racial composition of the provinces was barely changed. The inhabitants, whether they adopted Islam or remained Christian, soon adopted the Arabic tongue for all general purposes; and we now loosely call their descendants Arabs. In fact they were formed of a blend of many races, of tribes that had been in the land before ever Israel came out of Egypt, of later comers such as the Arameans, of settlers of many sorts who arrived under the Hellenistic rulers and the Romans, as well as the descendants of the Jews who had embraced Christianity. Only the practising Jews remained distinct. Arab immigration was thickest in areas bordering the desert and along the caravan routes. In the Hellenistic cities along the coast the Christian element remained strong. In Jerusalem itself the Christians, nearly all of them Orthodox, outnumbered the Moslems, as also in the holy cities of Bethlehem and Nazareth. There was a large Jewish colony in Jerusalem. There were other towns, such as Tiberias and Safed, which were almost exclusively Jewish. The Moslem administrative centre in Palestine was at Ramleh, on the coastal plain.

On the whole the Christians did not fare badly under Moslem rule, so long as they had no political ambitions. From AD 660, for nearly a century, the Caliphate was ruled by the Ommayad dynasty, whose capital was at Damascus. They were tolerant and cultured rulers who employed Christian clerks in their administration and Christian architects and artists for their buildings. When the Ommayads were overthrown by the Abbasid family, who moved the capital to Baghdad in Iraq, the Syro-Hellenistic influences gave way to influences of Persian origin. It was only in Spain, to which the Ommayads fled for refuge, that Hellenistic life lingered on in the Moslem world. The Abbasids were less tolerant than the Ommayads; and local Christians had little access to the Court, apart from the Nestorian scholars who translated old Greek works on philosophy and science for the Caliphs. There were at first some fierce anti-Christian riots, and there were unscrupulous governors in Syria and Palestine who victimized the Christians. But on the whole life continued to be orderly. Indeed, fanatical Moslem writers began to complain that the Christians were too prosperous.

After the failure of the Arabs to capture Constantinople, warfare between the Christian Empire and the Caliphate was confined to raids and skirmishes along the frontier, and occasionally to a larger expedition by the Caliph's army or, less often, by the Emperor's into enemy lands, with booty rather than conquest as its aim. Merchants passed over the frontiers with little interruption. Embassies were constantly exchanged between the two capitals. Both Constantinople and Baghdad were interested in each other's culture, especially in architecture and in the arts of elegant living. The two great cities were the undoubted capitals of civilization; and the Emperor regarded the Caliph, alone of the monarchs of the world, as being his equal.

In the course of the tenth century Abbasid power began rapidly to decline. In Syria local dynasties appeared, which paid little attention to Baghdad. By 970 Egypt was in the hands of a rival dynasty, the Fatimids, who had heretic Shia tendencies; and before the end of the century the Fatimids had occupied Palestine and southern Syria.

At the same time there was a remarkable revival of Byzantine power. The tide had turned by the middle of the tenth century, when Christian armies began to campaign in Syria. Then the warrior-Emperor Nicephorus II Phocus, in his brief reign from 963 to 969, recaptured Cilicia and the ancient metropolis of Antioch; and several great Moslem cities such as Aleppo became his vassals. His successor, John I Tzimisces, carried on the wars of conquest, annexing the Syrian coastlands almost as far as Tortosa; and in 974 he led his army right into Galilee. But his sudden death early in 976 halted the wars of conquest. The next Emperor, Basil II, though an even more brilliant soldier, was too badly distracted by civil war and then by war in the Balkans to do more than maintain the conquests. In 1001 he made a ten-year truce with the Fatimids which divided Syria between them, the frontier running from just north of Tortosa on the coast to just south of Shaizar in the Orontes valley. The truce was renewed in due course and remained in force for half a century.

The truce brought tranquillity and prosperity to the Christians in Palestine, except for a period of ten years, from 1004 to 1014, when the mad Fatimid Caliph Hakim, the son of a Christian mother, decided to persecute the Christians, ordering the destruction of a number of churches, including that of the Holy Sepulchre, and forcing many Christians to adopt Islam. The Emperor protested in vain: until Hakim decided that he was the incarnation of Allah and turned his persecuting zeal against the Moslems who would not accept him. Christians and Jews were restored to favour; and the converts were allowed to return to their old faith. In 1021 Hakim disappeared. He was probably murdered by his sister; but his corpse was never found. His chief adviser and supporter, Darazi, fled to the Lebanon, to found there the sect that is called the Druzes, after his name. They believe that in due course Hakim will come again.

In the long run the episode benefited the Christians. A treaty signed in 1027 and renewed in 1036 restored to them all their property and privileges and gave the Emperor the right of restoring the Holy Sepulchre. The work was carried out in the 1040s, when Jerusalem was so full of Byzantine officials that the Emperor seemed to have taken over the whole city. The restoration was financed by tolls raised by these officials on pilgrims.

In the mid-eleventh century the lot of the Christians in Palestine had seldom been so pleasant. The Fatimid authorities were lenient; the Emperor was watchful of their interests. Trade was prospering and increasing with Christian countries overseas. And never before had Jerusalem enjoyed so plentifully the wealth and sympathy brought to it by pilgrims from the West.

The pilgrims of Christ

Our feet shall stand within thy gates, O Jerusalem.

Psalms CXXII, 2

The desire to be a pilgrim is deeply rooted in human nature. To stand where those that we reverence once stood, to see the very sites where they were born and toiled and died, gives us a feeling of mystical contact with them and is a practical expression of our homage. And if the great men of the world have their shrines to which their admirers come from afar, still more do men flock eagerly to those places where, they believe, the Divine has sanctified the earth.

In the earliest days of Christianity pilgrimages were rare. Early Christian thought tended to emphasize the godhead and the universality of Christ rather than the manhood; and the Roman authorities did not encourage a voyage to Palestine. Jerusalem itself, destroyed by Titus, lay in ruins till Hadrian rebuilt it as the Roman city of Aelia. But the Christians remembered the setting of the drama of Christ's life. Their respect for the site of Calvary was such that Hadrian deliberately erected there a temple to Venus Capitolina. By the third century the cave at Bethlehem where Christ was born was well known to them; and Christians would journey thither and to the Mount of Olives, to the Garden of Gethsemane and to the place of the Ascension. A visit to such holy spots for the purpose of prayer and of acquiring spiritual merit was already a part of Christian practice.

With the triumph of the Cross the practice grew. The Emperor Constantine was glad to give strength to the religion that he had chosen. His mother, the Empress Helena, most exalted and most successful of the world's great archaeologists, set out to Palestine, to uncover Calvary and to find all the relics of the Passion. The Emperor endorsed her discovery by building there a church, which through all its vicissitudes has remained the chief sanctuary of Christendom, the Church of the Holy Sepulchre.

At once a stream of pilgrims began to flow to the scene of Helena's labours. We cannot tell their numbers; for most of them left no record of their journey. But already in 333, before her excavations were finished, a traveller who wrote of his voyage came all the way from Bordeaux to Palestine. Soon afterwards we find the description of a tour made by an indefatigable lady known sometimes as Aetheria and sometimes as Saint Silvia of Aquitaine. Towards the close of the century one of the great Fathers of Latin Christendom, Saint Jerome, settled in Palestine and drew after him the circle of rich and fashionable women that had sat at his feet in Italy. In his cell at Bethlehem he received a constant procession of travellers who came to pay him their respects after viewing the holy places. Saint Augustine, most spiritual of the western Fathers, considered pilgrimages to be irrelevant and even dangerous, and the Greek Fathers tended to agree with him; but Saint Jerome, though he did not maintain that actual residence in Jerusalem was of any spiritual value, asserted that it was an act of faith to pray where the feet of Christ had stood. His view was more popular than Augustine's. Pilgrimages multiplied, encouraged by the authorities. By the beginning of the next century there were said to be already two hundred monasteries and hospices in or around Jerusalem, built to receive pilgrims, and almost all under the patronage of the Emperor.

The mid-fifth century saw the height of this early taste for Jerusalem. The Empress Eudocia, born the daughter of a pagan philosopher at Athens, settled there after an unhappy life at Court; and many pious members of the Byzantine aristocracy came in her train. In the intervals of writing hymns she patronized the growing fashion for collecting relics; and she laid the foundation of the great collection at Constantinople by sending there the portrait of Our Lady painted by Saint Luke.

Her example was followed by pilgrims from the West as well
as from Constantinople. From immemorial ages the material
luxuries of the world came from the East. Now religious
luxuries too went westward. Christianity was at first an eastern
religion. The majority of the early Christian saints and martyrs
had been easterners. There was a spreading tendency to
venerate the saints. Authorities such as Prudentius and
Ennodius taught that divine succour could be found at their
graves and that their bodies should be able to work miracles.
Men and women would now travel far to see a holy relic. Still
more, they would try to acquire one, to take it home and to set
it in their local sanctuary. The chief relics remained in the East,
those of Christ at Jerusalem till they were moved to
Constantinople, and those of the saints for the most part at their
native places. But minor relics began to penetrate to the West,
brought by some lucky pilgrim or some enterprising merchant,
or sent as a gift to some potentate. Soon there followed small
portions of major relics, then major relics in their entirety. All
this helped to draw the attention of the West to the East. The
citizens of Langres, proud possessors of a finger of Saint
Mamas, would inevitably wish to visit Caesarea in Cappadocia
where the saint had lived. The nuns of Chamalières, with the
bones of Thecla in their chapel, would take a personal interest
in her birthplace at Isaurian Seleucia. When a lady of
Maurienne brought back from her travels the thumb of Saint
John the Baptist, her friends were all inspired to journey out to
see his body at Samaria and his head at Damascus. Whole
embassies would be sent in the hope of securing some such
treasure, maybe even a phial of the Holy Blood or a fragment
of the true Cross itself. Churches were built in the West called
after eastern saints or after the Holy Sepulchre; and often a
portion of their revenues was set aside to be sent to the holy
places from which they took their names.

This interconnection was helped by the commerce that was
still kept up round the coasts of the Mediterranean. It was
slowly declining, owing to the growing impoverishment of the
West; and at times it was interrupted, as when the Vandal
pirates in the mid-fifth century made the seas no longer safe for
unarmed traders; and discontent and heresy in the East added

further difficulties. But there are many itineraries written in the sixth century by western pilgrims who had travelled eastward in Greek or Syrian merchant ships; and the merchants themselves carried religious news and gossip as well as passengers and merchandise. Thanks to the travellers and the traders, the historian Gregory of Tours was well informed on Oriental affairs. There exists the record of a conversation between Saint Symeon Stylites and a Syria merchant who saw him on his pillar near Aleppo, in which Saint Symeon asked for news of Saint Geneviève of Paris and sent her a personal message. In spite of the religious and political quarrels of the higher authorities, the relations between eastern and western Christians remained very cordial and close.

With the Arab conquests this era came to an end. Syrian merchants no longer came to the coasts of France and Italy, bringing their wares and their news. There were pirates again in the Mediterranean. The Moslem rulers of Palestine were suspicious of Christian travellers from abroad. The journey was expensive and difficult; and there was little wealth left in western Christendom. But intercourse was not entirely broken off. Western Christians still thought of the eastern holy places with sympathy and longing. When, in 682, Pope Martin I was accused of friendly dealing with the Moslems, he explained that his motive was to seek permission to send alms to Jerusalem. In 670 the Frankish bishop Arculf set out for the East and managed to make a complete tour of Egypt, Syria and Palestine, and to return through Constantinople; but the journey took several years, and he met with many hardships. We know the names of other pilgrims of the time, such as Vulphy of Rue in Picardy, or Bercaire of Montier-en-Der in Burgundy and his friend Waimer. But their stories showed that only rough and enterprising men could hope to reach Jerusalem. No women seem to have ventured on the pilgrimage.

During the eighth century the number of pilgrims increased. Some even came from England; of whom the most famous was Willibald, who died in 781 as Bishop of Eichstadt in Bavaria. In his youth he had gone to Palestine, leaving Rome in 722 and only returning there, after many disagreeable adventures, in

729. Towards the end of the century there seems to have been an attempt to organize pilgrimages, under the patronage of Charles the Great. Charles had restored order and some prosperity to the West and had established good relations with the Caliph Harun al-Rashid. The hostels that were erected by his help in the Holy Land show that in his time many pilgrims must have reached Jerusalem, and women amongst them. Nuns from Christian Spain were sent to serve at the Holy Sepulchre. But this activity was shortlived. The Carolingian empire declined. Moslem pirates reappeared in the eastern Mediterranean; Norse pirates came in from the West. When Bernard the Wise, from Brittany, visited Palestine in 870, he found Charles's establishments still in working order, but empty and beginning to decay. Bernard had only been able to make the journey by obtaining a passport from the Moslem authorities then governing Bari, in southern Italy; and even this passport did not enable him to land at Alexandria.

The great age of Pilgrimage begins with the tenth century. The Arabs lost their last pirate-nests in Italy and southern France in the course of the century; and Crete was taken from them in 961. Already by then the Byzantine navy had been for some time sufficiently in command of the seas for maritime commerce in the Mediterranean to have fully revived. Greek and Italian merchant ships sailed freely between the ports of Italy and the Empire and were beginning, with the goodwill of the Moslem authorities, to open up trade with Syria and Egypt. It was easy for a pilgrim to secure a passage direct from Venice or from Bari to Tripoli or Alexandria; though most travellers preferred to call in at Constantinople to see its great collections of relics and then to proceed by sea or by the land route, which recent Byzantine military successes had now made secure. In Palestine itself the Moslem authorities, whether Abbasid, Ikshid or Fatimid, seldom caused difficulties, but, rather, welcomed the travellers for the wealth that they brought into the province.

The improvement in the conditions of pilgrimage had its effect on western religious thought. It is doubtful at what age pilgrimages were first ordered as canonical penances. Early medieval *poenitentialia* all recommend a pilgrimage, but usually without giving a specified goal. But the belief was growing that certain holy places possessed a definite spiritual virtue which affected those that visited them and could even grant indulgences from sin. Thus the pilgrim knew that not only would he be able to pay reverence to the earthly remains and surroundings of God and His saints and so enter into mystical contact with them but he might also obtain God's pardon for his wickedness. From the tenth century onwards four shrines in particular were held to have this power: those of Saint James at Compostella in Spain and of Saint Michael at Monte Gargano in Italy, the many sacred sites at Rome, and, above all, the holy places in Palestine. To all of these access was now far easier, owing to the retreat or the goodwill of the Moslems. But the journey was still sufficiently long and arduous to appeal to the common sense as well as to the religious feeling of medieval man. It was wise to remove a criminal for the space of a year or more from the scene of his crime. The discomforts and expense of his journey would be a punishment to him, while the achievement of his task and the emotional atmosphere of his goal would give him a feeling of spiritual cleansing and strength. He returned a better man.

Casual references in the chroniclers tell us of frequent pilgrimages though the names of the actual pilgrims that we now possess are inevitably only those of the greater personages. From amongst the great lords and ladies of the West there came Hilda, Countess of Swabia, who died on her journey in 969, and Judith, Duchess of Bavaria, sister-in-law of the Emperor Otto I, whose tour took place in 970. The Counts of Ardèche, of Vienne, of Verdun, of Arcy, of Anhalt and of Gorizia, all were pilgrims. Leading ecclesiastics were even more assiduous. Saint Conrad, Bishop of Constance, made three separate journeys to Jerusalem, and Saint John, Bishop of Parma, no less than six. The Bishop of Olivola was there in 920. Pilgrim abbots included those of Saint-Cybar, of Flavigny, of Aurillac, of Saint-Aubin d'Angers and of Montier-en-Der. All these eminent travellers brought with them groups of humble men and women whose names were of no interest to the writers of the time.

This activity was mainly the result of private enterprise. But a new force was appearing in European politics, which amongst its other work set about the organization of the pilgrim traffic. In 910 Count William I of Aquitaine founded the Abbey of Cluny. By the end of the century Cluny, ruled by a series of remarkable abbots, was the centre of a vast ecclesiastical nexus, well ordered, closely knit and intimately connected with the Papacy. The Cluniacs regarded themselves as the keepers of the conscience of western Christendom. Their doctrine approved of pilgrimage. They wished to give it practical assistance. By the beginning of the next century the pilgrimages to the great Spanish shrines were almost entirely under their control. At the same time they began to arrange and to popularize journeys to Jerusalem. It was owing to their persuasion that the Abbot of Stavelot set out for the Holy Land in 990 and the Count of Verdun in 997. Their influence is shown by the great increase in the eleventh century of pilgrims from France and Lorraine, from districts that were near to Cluny and her daughter houses. Though there were still many Germans amongst the pilgrims of the eleventh century, such as the Archbishops of Trier and Mainz and the Bishop of Bamberg, and many pilgrims from England, French and Lorraine pilgrims now by far outnumbered them. The two great dynasties of northern France, the Counts of Anjou and the Dukes of Normandy, were both, despite their mutual rivalry, the close friends of Cluny; and both patronized the eastern journey. The terrible Fulk Nerra of Anjou went to Jerusalem in 1002 and twice returned there later. Duke Richard III of Normandy sent alms there, and Duke Robert led a huge company there in 1035. All these pilgrimages were faithfully recorded by the Cluniac historian, the monk Glaber.

The Normans followed their Dukes' example. They had a particular veneration for Saint Michael; and great numbers of them made the journey to Monte Gargano. From there the more enterprising would go on to Palestine. In the middle of the century they formed so large and so fervent a proportion of the Palestine pilgrims that the government at Constantinople, angry with the Normans for their raids on Byzantine Italy, began to show some ill-will towards the pilgrim traffic. Their cousins from Scandinavia showed an almost equal enthusiasm. Scandinavians had long been used to visit Constantinople; and its wealth and wonders greatly impressed them. They talked in their northern homes of Micklegarth, as they called the great city; which they even at times identified with Asgard, the home of the gods. Already by 930 there were Norsemen in the Emperor's army. Early in the eleventh century there were so many of them that a special Norse regiment was formed, the famed Varangian Guard. The Varangians soon acquired the habit of spending a leave on a journey to Jerusalem. The first of whom we have a record was a certain Kolskeggr, who was in Palestine in 992. Harald Hardrada, most famous of the Varangians, was there in 1034. During the eleventh century there were many Norwegians, Icelanders and Danes who spent five or more years in the imperial service, then made the pilgrimage before they returned, rich with their savings, to their homes in the north. Stimulated by their tales their friends would come south merely to make the pilgrimage. The apostle to Iceland, Thorvald Kódransson Vidtförli, was in Jerusalem about the year 990. Several Norse pilgrims claimed to have seen there Olaf Tryggvason, first Christian king of Norway, after his mysterious disappearance in 1000. Olaf II intended to follow his example, but his voyage never took place except in legend. These Nordic princes were violent men, frequently guilty of murder and frequently in need of an act of penance. The half-Danish Swein Godwinsson set out with a body of Englishmen in 1051 to expiate a murder, but died of exposure in the Anatolian mountains next autumn. He had gone barefoot because of his sins. Lagman Gudrödsson, Norse king of Man, who had slain his brother, sought a similar pardon from God. Most Scandinavian pilgrims liked to make a round tour, coming by sea through the Straits of Gibraltar and returning overland through Russia.

Tenth-century pilgrims from the West had been obliged to travel by sea across the Mediterranean to Constantinople or to Syria. But fares were high and berths not easy to obtain. In 975 the rulers of Hungary were converted to Christianity; and an overland route was opened, going down the Danube and across the Balkans to Constantinople. Till 1019, when Byzantium finally established control over the whole Balkan peninsula, this was a dangerous road; but thenceforward a pilgrim could travel with very little risk through Hungary to cross the Byzantine frontier at Belgrade and then proceed through Sofia and Adrianople to the capital. Alternatively, he could now go to Byzantine Italy and make the short sea-passage across from Bari to Dyrrhachium and then follow the old Roman Via Egnatia through Thessalonica to the Bosphorus. There were three good main roads that would take him across Asia Minor to Antioch. Thence he went down to the coast at Lattakieh and crossed into Fatimid territory near Tortosa. This was the only frontier that he had to pass since his arrival at Belgrade or at Termoli in Italy; and he could proceed without further hindrance to Jerusalem. Travel overland, though slow, was far cheaper and easier than travel by sea, and far better suited to large companies.

So long as the pilgrims were orderly they could count ón hospitable treatment from the peasants of the Empire; and for the earlier part of their journey the Cluniacs were now building hostels along the route. There were several hospices in Italy, some restricted to the use of Norsemen. There was a great hospice at Melk in Austria. At Constantinople the Hospice of Samson was reserved for the use of western pilgrims; and the Cluniacs kept up an establishment at Rodosto in the suburbs. At Jerusalem itself pilgrims could stay at the Hospital of St John, founded by the merchants of Amalfi. There was no objection to the great lords of the West bringing with them an armed escort, so long as it was properly under control; and most pilgrims tried to join some such company. But it was not uncommon, nor particularly risky, for men to travel alone or in twos and threes. At times there might be difficulties. During Hakim's persecution it was uncomfortable to stay long in Palestine, though the flow of pilgrims was never wholly interrupted. In 1055 it was considered dangerous to cross the frontier into Moslem territory. Lietbert, Bishop of Cambrai, was not granted an exit-visa by the governor of Lattakieh and was forced to go to Cyprus. In 1056 the Moslems, perhaps with the connivance of the Emperor, forbade westerners to enter the Holy Sepulchre and ejected some three hundred of them from Jerusalem. Both Basil II and his niece the Empress Theodora caused offence by ordering their customs officers to levy a tax on pilgrims and their horses. Pope Victor II wrote to the Empress in December 1056, begging her to cancel the order; and his letter suggests that her officials were also to be found in Jerusalem itself.

But such inconveniences were rare. Throughout the eleventh century till its last two decades, an unending stream of travellers poured eastward, sometimes travelling in parties numbering thousands, men and women of every age and every class, ready, in that leisurely age, to spend a year or more on the voyage. They would pause at Constantinople to admire the huge city, ten times greater than any city that they knew in the West, and to pay reverence to the relics that it housed. They could see there the Crown of Thorns, the Seamless Garment and all the major relics of the Passion. There was the cloth from Edessa on which Christ had imprinted His face, and Saint Luke's own portrait of the Virgin; the hair of John the Baptist and the mantle of Elijah; the bodies of innumerable saints, prophets and martyrs; an endless store of the holiest things in Christendom. Thence they went on to Palestine, to Nazareth and Mount Tabor, to the Jordan and to Bethlehem, and to all the shrines of Jerusalem. They gazed at them all and prayed at them all; then they made the long voyage homeward, returning edified and purified, to be greeted by their countrymen as the pilgrims of Christ who had made the most sacred of journeys.

But the success of the pilgrimage depended on two conditions: first, that life in Palestine should be orderly enough for the defenceless traveller to move and worship in safety; and secondly, that the way should be kept open and cheap. The former necessitated peace and good government in the Moslem world, the latter the prosperity and benevolence of Byzantium.

CHAPTER 3

Confusion in the East

In prosperity the destroyer shall come.

Job xv, 21

In the middle of the eleventh century the tranquillity of the east
Mediterranean world seemed assured for many years to come.
Its two great powers, Byzantium and Fatimid Egypt, were on
good terms with each other. Neither was aggressive; both
wished to keep in check the Moslem states further to the east,
where adventurers from Turkestan were stirring up trouble,
which as yet did not seem serious. The Fatimids showed
goodwill towards the local Christians and welcomed merchants
and pilgrims from the West; and this goodwill was guaranteed
by the power of Byzantium.

Thanks to a series of great warrior-Emperors the Byzantine
Empire now stretched from the Lebanon to the Danube and
from Naples to the Caspian Sea. Despite occasional corruption
and an occasional riot it was better administered than any
other contemporary state. Constantinople had never before
been so wealthy. It was the financial and commercial capital of
the world. Traders from western and northern Europe and
from Africa and the East came crowding there to exchange
their wares and to buy the luxuries that its factories produced.
The bustling life of the vast city, far richer and more populous
now than Baghdad or Cairo, never failed to amaze the traveller
with its crowded harbour, its full bazaars, its wide suburbs and
its superb churches and palaces. It was full of artists and of
scholars, and dominated by a magnificent Court which seemed
to be the centre of the world.

But the foundations of the Empire were insecure. It had been organized for defence. The provinces were governed by military officials, themselves controlled by the civil administration at Constantinople. The system provided a local militia that could defend the district in times of invasion and could supplement the main imperial army on its great campaigns. The land particularly in Anatolia, was largely occupied by free peasant villages which provided the Empire with most of its soldiers. But now the days of raids and invasions were over. Land was a good investment, eagerly desired by successful ministers or generals or wealthy merchants. The provincial governor tended to become a local magnate; and a landed aristocracy arose which began to take over the free villages, either by direct purchase or by offering to pay the villagers' taxes for them in return for their services. The tenth-century Emperors had vainly tried to control the growth of landed estates by legislation. At the end of the century, Basil II had had to defeat two successive revolts by landed magnates. His prestige kept the Imperial Court in control so long as his dynasty lasted. But in 1056 his niece, the aged spinster Empress Theodora, died without any heir. There followed a struggle for the control of the Imperial throne between the civil servants who controlled the central government and the landed magnates who controlled the army. Theodora was succeeded by a decrepit civil servant, who soon lost the throne to a leading general, Isaac Comnenus. But Isaac found the ill-will of the civil service too much for him. After two years he retired to a monastery, nominating as his successor a leading magnate who had made his career at Court and who might therefore be acceptable to both parties.

The new Emperor, Constantine Ducas, was, however, unfaithful to his caste. He saw that the army was dangerously powerful. His solution was to reduce the armed forces and to rely, should it be necessary, on mercenaries dependent on himself for their pay. At any time it would have been dangerous to weaken the defence of the Empire. At this juncture it was to prove disastrous. Storm clouds were gathering in the East; and in the West a storm had broken.

The frontier of the Byzantine Empire in southern Italy ran officially from Terracina on the Tyrrhenian Sea to Termoli on the Adriatic. Within that line only the provinces of Apulia and Calabria, both of them mainly Greek-speaking, were under the direct rule of Byzantium. On the west coast were three autonomous merchant-cities, Gaeta, Naples and Amalfi, all under the nominal suzerainty of the Emperor; and in the case of Amalfi, which already had wide commercial interests in the Near East and found the protection of the Emperor very useful there, the suzerainty was fully acknowledged. The interior was held by the Lombard Princes of Benevento and Salerno, who offered allegiance to Byzantium when it suited them. Sicily had been held by the Moslems since the late ninth century, despite several Byzantine attempts to recover the island.

Into these districts had come large numbers of Norman adventurers from northern France, pilgrims on their way to Jerusalem or to visit their favourite shrine of St Michael on Monte Gargano in the north of Apulia. Many were soldiers of fortune who stayed on to serve the Lombard princes. There was a land-hunger in Normandy whose thickly populated estates offered no scope for younger sons. This impulse for expansion, which was soon to make them undertake the conquest of England, turned their eyes towards the East. They saw southern Italy as the key to a Mediterranean Empire. Its confusion gave them their opportunity.

In 1040 six brothers, the sons of a petty Norman knight, Tancred de Hauteville, seized the town of Melfi in the Apulian hills. The Byzantines did not take them seriously; but they were encouraged by the western Emperor, who was always jealous of his eastern rival, and by the Pope whom he had appointed. Within twelve years they had established a mastery over the Lombard principalities. They had driven the Byzantines to the coast and were threatening the cities on the west coast; and they were beginning to raid into Papal territory. Both the Byzantines and the new Pope, Leo IX, were alarmed and in 1053 they decided on joint action. But before the Byzantine army could reach him, the Pope's army was routed at Civitate and the Pope himself captured. To obtain his release, he

disavowed his former policy. In 1059 his successor, ˙Pope
Nicholas II, recognized the eldest survivor of the Hauteville
brothers, Robert Guiscard, or 'the weasel', as 'Duke of Apulia
and Calabria, by the grace of God and Saint Peter, and, with
their help, of Sicily'. This recognition, considered by Rome but
not by Robert, to involve vassaldom to Saint Peter's heir,
enabled the Normans easily to finish off the conquest. By 1060
all that was left to Byzantium in Italy was the old capital of the
province, the coastal fortress of Bari. Meanwhile the youngest
Hauteville brother, Roger, had begun his slow conquest of
Sicily from the Arabs.

So long as Bari held out there was some check on further
Norman expansion. The Byzantines abandoned any hope of
reconquest. Their attention was fixed on far worse dangers
threatening from the East.

The Turks had long played an important role in history. The
Turkish Empire of the sixth century had been a civilized force
in Asia during its short life. Outlying Turkish peoples, such as
the Judaistic Khazars on the Volga or the Nestorian Christian
Ouigours on the boundaries of China, showed themselves to be
capable of cultural progress. But in Turkestan itself the
population was still pastoral and semi-nomadic. It was however
rapidly increasing, in a land that was becoming more and more
desiccated.

In the tenth century Turkestan was ruled by a Persian
dynasty, the Samanids, who converted their subjects to Islam.
They were succeeded by the first great Moslem Turk, Mahmud
the Ghaznavid, who in the early eleventh century built up an
empire which stretched from Ispahan to Bokhara and Lahore.
In the meantime Turkish adventurers were pouring into
western Asia to take service under various Moslem rulers.
Before the end of the tenth century the Caliph at Baghdad had
a Turkish bodyguard.

Amongst these adventurers was a group of princes who
called themselves Seldjuk, after a common semi-mythical
ancestor. They were jealous of each other but ready to
cooperate to advance the family, not unlike the Hauteville
brothers; but, luckier than the Normans, whose followers were

few, they had the support of vast, restless hordes of Turcomans. After Mahmud's death in 1030 they seized his Iranian territories; and in 1055 the Abbasid Caliph invited the head of the clan, Tughril Bey, to come to Baghdad, to take over the secular government of the Caliphate, with the title of King of the East and the West.

The Turks had already begun to make raids into Armenia; and to coordinate the defence the Byzantines annexed the Armenian principalities one by one, to the resentment of the Armenians. Tughril Bey died in 1063. Under his nephew and heir, Alp Arslan, the raids intensified. Alp Arslan saw the heretic Fatimids as his chief enemy. He feared a Fatimid-Byzantine alliance; and the raids were intended to distract Byzantium. But behind the raiders were Turcoman hordes, eager for new lands in which to settle. In 1064 the last independent Armenian ruler gladly handed over his lands to the Emperor in return for lands in the Taurus mountains. Large numbers of Armenians followed him to his new home; and others fled from the raids into the mountains of the Anti-Taurus. By 1070 Turkish raiders had penetrated into the heart of Anatolia, almost reaching the Aegean coast.

Byzantium had to take action. Constantine Ducas, whose policy of reducing the armed forces was largely responsible for the present danger, had died in 1067, leaving a young son as his heir. In 1068 the Empress-Mother prudently married the leading army commander, Romanus Diogenes, creating him Emperor-Regent till the boy should grow up. In 1071, hearing that Alp Arslan was gathering a large army, Romanus decided to strike first and to attack the Turks through Armenia. His army was huge by medieval standards, but its quality was poor. Owing to the recent economies it was composed mainly of mercenaries, the Norsemen of the Imperial Varangian Guard, heavy cavalry from the West under a Norman leader, Roussel of Bailleul, and large numbers of Cumans, Turks from the Russian steppes. Alp Arslan, who had intended to use his army against the Fatimids in Syria, hurried northward to meet the Emperor. On Friday 19 August, Romanus was in a narrow valley near to the town of Manzikert, waiting to be rejoined by

the bulk of his mercenary troops, which he had sent off to
secure the nearby fortress of Akhlat. He had forgotten the first
rule of Byzantine tactics and had neglected to send out scouts.
Suddenly the Turkish army fell on him. The Cuman
mercenaries who were about to join him went over at once to
the enemy, remembering that they were fellow-Turks. The
Western mercenaries rode off and took no part in the battle.
Some of the Byzantine troops managed to escape before it was
too late, leaving the Emperor to his fate. The main Imperial
army was annihilated, and the Emperor himself taken prisoner.

The battle of Manzikert was the worst disaster to befall
Byzantium; and it was the indirect cause of the Crusades. For
ten years the Empire was in chaos. Alp Arslan himself did not
follow up his victory. But the Turcoman hordes soon discovered
that the defences of Anatolia were down; and they began to
pour into the peninsula. In 1073 Alp Arslan's son and successor,
Malik Shah, appointed his cousin, Suleiman ibn Kutulmish, as
Sultan of Rum – that is, of the Roman Empire – with the task
of conquering the country. The task was made easy by the
Byzantines themselves. The provincial Byzantine troops could
not contain the invaders. They retired to the coastlands,
followed by much of the Christian population. Constantinople
itself was distracted by intrigues around the throne. On the
news of Romanus Diogenes's captivity his stepson, Michael
Ducas, took over the government. He was a cultured, intelligent
youth who, in better times, might have been a good Emperor.
But the problems were too great for him. After seven unhappy
years, with the Turks advancing and his own generals
conspiring against him, he retired into a monastery, from
which he eventually emerged to become a popular and efficient
archbishop. His successor, Nicephorus Boteniates, controlled
the garrison in the capital but was not recognized by the
commanders of either the European or the Asiatic army. In the
meantime the European provinces were in danger. In 1071,
just before the Imperial army set out on the fatal march to
Manzikert, news reached Constantinople that Bari, the
Emperor's last possession in Italy, had fallen to the Normans.
The Emperor Michael accepted the loss of Byzantine Italy and

sought to be on good terms with Robert Guiscard. But when Michael fell from power, Guiscard crossed the Adriatic with a considerable army and marched on the great port of Dyrrhachium.

By 1080 the whole of Asia Minor was in Turkish hands except for the Black Sea coast and districts in the southwestern corner of the peninsula. Sultan Suleiman had penetrated to the Sea of Marmora and had established his capital in the venerable city of Nicaea, less than a hundred miles from Constantinople. His territory included most of the centre of the peninsula. On the Aegean coast a Turkish chieftain called Chaka had set up an emirate at Smyrna and built a fleet, which he used profitably for piracy. Further east the Danishmend family had founded an emirate; and there were other emirs to the south of the Danishmends. Most of them only recognized Malik Shah as their overlord. Further to the southeast the great city of Antioch was still nominally in Imperial hands, ruled till 1085, when it was captured by Sultan Suleiman, by an Imperial official of Armenian origin called Philaretus. Lieutenants of his held other cities along the borders of Syria, Marash, Melitene and Edessa, relying on the support of their many fellow Armenians who had fled to the Anti-Taurus mountains; while there were two Armenian principalities now in the Taurus mountains.

Under such circumstances it was impossible for pilgrims to cross Anatolia on their way to the Holy Land. Even if they managed to reach Palestine by sea they found things little better there. Turkish adventurers had begun to invade Syria about the same time as Anatolia; but their followers were fewer. They did not manage to dislodge all the Arab princes. They managed, however, to bring Fatimid domination to an end. In 1071, the year of the battle of Manzikert, a Turkish chieftain, Atsiz ibn Abaq, invaded Palestine and captured Jerusalem without a struggle. Five years later he added Damascus to his dominions. In 1076 the Fatimids recovered Jerusalem, and Atsiz called in a Seldjuk prince, Tutush, the brother of Malik Shah, to help him. Tutush soon arranged for Atsiz's murder and by 1079 was ruler of all Syria south of

Aleppo, with his lieutenant Ortoq as his viceroy in Jerusalem. Between them they established a fairly orderly state in the cities. But the roads were still infested by bandits; and local lords exacted tolls from passers-by.

In 1081 the throne at Constantinople was taken over by a young general, Alexius Comnenus, who was to reign for thirty-seven years and to prove the greatest statesman of his time. Though he was barely thirty he had had many years' experience as a general, whose successes had depended on his wits and his diplomacy. His appearance was impressive; he was not tall but well-built, with a dignified air. He was gracious in manner, with remarkable self-control. He combined a genuine kindliness with a cynical readiness to use trickery and terror in the interests of his country. His only assets were his personal qualities and the affection of his troops. His family connections, which branched through the whole Byzantine aristocracy, certainly helped him to gain power. But the intrigues and jealousies of his relations and of the members of former Imperial families or of the families of would-be usurpers, together with the unreliability of the senior civil service, led to endless conspiracies against his government; and he was in constant danger of assassination. His clemency and calmness were remarkable in view of the insecurity in which his whole life was spent.

The state of the Empire in 1081 was such that only a man of great courage or great stupidity would have undertaken its government. The treasury was empty. Recent Emperors had been spendthrift. The loss of Anatolia and rebellions in Europe had seriously diminished the revenue. The old system of tax collection had broken down. Alexius was no financier. His methods would have left a modern economist aghast. Yet somehow, by taxing his subjects to the utmost, exacting forced loans and confiscating property from the magnates and the Church, punishing with fines rather than with imprisonment, selling privileges, and developing the Palace industries, he managed to pay for a large administrative service and to rebuild the army and the navy; and, despite his own simple personal tastes, he maintained a sumptuous and lavishly generous Court, being well aware that in the East prestige depends upon magnificence. But he made two great errors. In return for immediate aid he gave commercial privileges to foreign merchants, to the detriment of his own subjects; and at one crucial moment he debased the imperial coinage, which for seven centuries had been the one stable currency in a chaotic world.

Alexius had at once to decide against which of his foreign enemies he should first campaign. He calculated that he was not yet ready to take on the Turks. In the meantime their chieftains were quarrelling amongst themselves; and he used diplomatic means to encourage their quarrels. The Normans from southern Italy were a more immediate menace. Robert Guiscard, accompanied by his eldest son, Bohemond, landed with an army in Epirus in the summer of 1081. The Emperor, aided by the Venetian navy, had at first little success in driving them out. The chief regiment in his army, the Varangian Guard, was now composed mainly of Anglo-Saxon refugees from England, as he could no longer trust Norsemen to fight against their Norman cousins. But the Anglo-Saxons were no more successful at Dyrrhachium against the Normans than they had been at Hastings fifteen years previously. It was only in 1085, when Robert Guiscard died and Bohemond hurried back to Italy to fight with his brothers over the inheritance, that Alexius was able to re-establish his authority over his European provinces. Soon afterwards he had to meet a serious invasion by Petcheneg barbarians from over the Danube; but by 1091 he was securely in control of the Balkans.

By then he had begun to take a more aggressive line against the Turks. In 1085 he recovered the Bithynian coastline of the Sea of Marmora. In 1086 Sultan Suleiman was killed fighting against his cousin Tutush for the control of Aleppo. For the next five years Turkish princes fought for the inheritance until Suleiman's son, Kilij Arslan I, established himself in Nicaea; but he was in no position now to threaten Constantinople. More dangerous was the Emir Chaka of Smyrna who, with the help of Greek sailors, was spreading his dominion along the Aegean coast and over the islands of Lesbos, Chios, Samos and

Rhodes. It was with his help that Kilij Arslan, who had married his daughter, had managed to recover Nicaea from an usurper. But Alexius managed to stir up trouble between Kilij Arslan and his son-in-law, who was murdered at a banquet in Nicaea in 1092. His son, the younger Chaka, was too busy trying to hold his inheritance together to venture on further aggression.

By 1095 Alexius was ready to contemplate action against the Turks. For the moment his European lands were quiet; and in Asia the Seldjuk power was declining. Malik Shah died in 1092, Tutush in 1095; and Tutush's sons, Ridwan of Aleppo and Duqaq of Damascus, were fighting against each other or against the atabeg of Mosul, Kerbogha, the most formidable of the younger Turkish chieftains. In Palestine the Fatimids were advancing against the sons of Ortoq. The Anatolian Turks would get little support from their kinsmen in Syria. But Alexius was short of manpower. He needed recruits for his army. His finances were in better order; he could afford to hire mercenaries, and the best mercenaries came from the West.

Meanwhile the pilgrim traffic from the West was almost at a standstill. Count Robert I of Flanders managed to make his way to Jerusalem in 1086, with the help of a large armed escort. He paused on the way back to spend a season fighting for the Emperor. But the few humbler pilgrims who succeeded in overcoming all the difficulties returned to their homes weary and impoverished, with a doleful tale to tell.

CHAPTER 4

Holy peace and holy war

We looked for peace, but no good came.

Jeremiah VIII, 15

The Christian citizen has a fundamental problem to face: is he entitled to fight for his country? His religion is a religion of peace; and war means slaughter and destruction. The earlier Christian Fathers had no doubts. To them a war was wholesale murder. But when the Empire became the Christian Empire, ought not its citizens to be ready to take up arms for its welfare?

The Eastern Church thought not. Its great canonist, Saint Basil, while he realized that the soldier must obey orders, yet maintained that anyone guilty of killing in war should refrain for three years from taking communion as a sign of repentance. This counsel was too strict. The Byzantine soldier was not treated as a murderer. But his profession brought him no glamour. Death in battle was not considered glorious; and death in battle against the infidel was not martyrdom; the martyr died armed only with his faith. Heraclius's war to recover the True Cross had been regarded as a holy task. But the Byzantine Church always refused to give a special blessing to a campaign against the infidel. Indeed, the Byzantine always preferred peaceful methods, as being morally better and usually materially cheaper, even if they involved tortuous diplomacy and the payment of money. War was a last resort, almost a confession of failure.

To Westerners, brought up to admire martial valour, the Byzantine desire to avoid bloodshed seemed cowardly and sly. The Western theologians were less strict. Saint Augustine held

33

that wars might be waged at the command of God; and the military society that had emerged in the West out of the barbarian invasions inevitably sought to justify its habitual pastime. The code of chivalry that was developing gave prestige to the military hero; and the pacifist acquired a disrepute from which he has never recovered. The Church could only try to divert this military energy into paths that were to its advantage. A war in the interests of the Church became a holy war, permissable and even desirable. Pope Leo IV in the mid-ninth century declared that anyone dying in battle for the Church would win a heavenly reward. Pope John VIII a few years later ranked soldiers dying in a holy war as martyrs whose sins would be forgiven, though they should be pure at heart. Pope Nicholas I held that men under the sentence of the Church for their sins might only bear arms against the infidel.

Unfortunately, most of the fighting of the time was between Christians, monarchs fighting against rival monarchs or, more frequently and more shamefully, local lords fighting against their neighbours. By the end of the tenth century this lawlessness was so great that local bishops, with the approval of various magnates and the support of the populace, tried to outlaw war and to found Leagues of Peace. But it is difficult ever to enforce peace. When in 1038 the Archbishop of Bourges ordered every Christian man over the age of fifteen to declare himself the enemy of anyone who broke the peace and if need be take up arms against him, his command was too fully obeyed. Castles of recalcitrant nobles were destroyed by troops of armed peasants led by the clergy; and this improvised militia soon became so irresponsibly destructive that the authorities were obliged to suppress it. After a League of Peace had burnt down the whole village of Bénécy, the Count of Déols routed it on the banks of the river Cher. Seven hundred clerics perished in the battle.

A more practical attempt to limit warfare was the proclamation of a Truce of God, which prohibited fighting on the sabbath and later on all the major feast days of the Church, and then extended to cover Saturdays as well as Sundays, and the

periods between Advent and Epiphany and between Ash
Wednesday and the octave of Easter. The Church in Burgundy
tried to permit fighting only between Monday mornings and
Wednesday evenings. Many princes subscribed to the Truce of
God, but few kept to it. William the Conqueror was an
enthusiastic advocate; but it was on a Saturday that he fought
against King Harold at Hastings.

Eventually the Church reverted to its older policy. The
fighting spirit of the Western knights should be directed against
the infidel and the heathen.

The Byzantines had long been used to the Moslems. They
recognized the civilization of the Caliphate as being on a level
with their own. They would have felt far more at home in Cairo
or Baghdad than in Paris or Aachen or even Rome. But to the
Western world the Moslems were strange and terrible. They
were firmly installed in Spain. Moslem pirates dominated the
western Mediterranean. There were Moslem robber castles in
Provence and Italy till the late tenth century. In 846 Moslems
had sacked Rome itself, and even in the first years of the
eleventh century they sacked Antibes, Pisa and Narbonne.
During the ninth century the Christians had won back much of
northern Spain, and the route to the shrine of Saint James at
Compostella had been safe for pilgrims. But in the late tenth
century there had been a revival of Moslem power under the
formidable vizier of Cordova, Mahomet ibn Abi Amir,
surnamed al-Mansur, the Victorious, and known to the
Spaniards as Almanzor. He had captured Zamora and
Barcelona, sacked Leon, the capital of the leading Christian
kingdom, and Compostella itself, though he respected the
shrine. But he died in 1001; and organized Moslem aggression
ceased. It was time for a counter-attack.

For this counter-attack the Christian Spanish princes sought
the help of the Church and, in particular, the great monastic
organization of Cluny, which was interested in pilgrimage and
eager to ensure the safety of pilgrims bound for Compostella.
The Cluniacs eagerly encouraged princes and knights from
France and Lorraine to fight against the infidel in Spain; and
when, in the mid-eleventh century, Cluniac influence became

dominant at the Papal Court, the Popes gave their blessing to the war. Pope Alexander II in 1064 offered an indulgence to anyone who went campaigning in Spain. Pope Gregory VII only gave absolution to all who died fighting for the Cross; but he also allowed the campaigners to take possession of the lands that they conquered, under the ultimate suzerainty of the Papacy. The war in Spain thus became a holy war, a Crusade, with the Pope usually naming the commander of the expedition. The knights who fought in it could satisfy their restlessness, their love of fighting, and their land-hunger, which was increasing as primogeniture became the rule in France; and at the same time they were doing God's work. To combine Christian duty with the acquisition of land in a southern climate was very attractive. Could it not be applied to the eastern frontier of Christendom?

The idea of a holy war directed by the Papacy was very attractive too to the great reforming pontiffs of the mid-eleventh century. The Papacy had recently escaped from the domination of western Emperors from Germany. It was anxious to establish its authority over the whole Church and its independence from all lay control and, indeed, its superiority over all lay potentates. It wished to ensure uniformity in creed, in liturgical usage and in discipline. These claims were not, however, acceptable to the Christians of the East. To the Orthodox Churches of the East the Emperor was the viceroy of God, responsible for the welfare of all Christians on earth. Doctrine could only be decided by an Oecumenical Council summoned by the Emperor, at which, ideally, all the bishops of Christendom be present. Administration and discipline in the Church were in the hands of the five great Patriarchates, of which the see of Rome had the primacy of honour but no authority over the fellow sees, the Patriarchates of Constantinople, Alexandria, Antioch and Jerusalem. The last three were now in the power of infidel rulers, against whom they depended on the Emperor and the Patriarch of Constantinople for succour. The Bishop of Rome, the heir of Saint Peter, enjoyed a special prestige; and the Emperors had at times made use of it to repress over-exuberant Patriarchs of Constantinople. But

Rome was now a paltry city, not to be compared with Constantinople, the undoubted capital of the Christian Empire. There was a fundamental difference in language. Rome insisted on Latin, while the Orthodox Churches, while mostly Greek-speaking, allowed the use of vernacular tongues in the liturgy. Different liturgical usages had arisen; and recently the Orthodox had been deeply shocked to find that, under German influence, Rome had inserted the word *filioque* in the Creed to describe the procession of the Holy Ghost, thus altering the inspired decision of the Second Oecumenical Council. Byzantium was also annoyed that the Papacy had given support to the Normans in Italy and had insisted that the Greek churches in the provinces conquered by the Normans should comply with Roman usages.

There had been periods before when Rome and Constantinople had broken off religious relations. But the quarrels had been patched up. No one wished to challenge the notion that Christendom was and should be united. In January 1054, on the invitation of the Emperor, Constantine IX, legates from Pope Leo IX arrived in Constantinople to settle the disputes. Unfortunately the Patriarch of Constantinople, Michael Cerularius, was an arrogant and ambitious man, while the chief Papal legate, Cardinal Humbert, was stubborn and equally arrogant, and became more obstinate when news reached him in April of the Pope's death which automatically cancelled his legatine powers. At last, after angry scenes, he departed for home leaving on the altar of the church of Saint Sophia a Bull excommunicating the Patriarch and his advisers. The Patriarch retorted by holding a synod which condemned the Cardinal as an irresponsible man who supported incorrect doctrine and usages. The episode is usually but wrongly held to mark the final schism between the Latin and Greek Churches. In fact neither side condemned more than individual clerics. Their respective Churches were clearly omitted from the condemnation. Moreover, the other Patriarchates of the East took no part in the quarrel.

Good relations were restored under the Emperor Michael VII, who made peace with the Normans and sought the friendship of the great Pope Gregory VII. A Papal legate visited Constantinople in 1074 and was well received there; and on his return he reported to Gregory about the difficulties that pilgrims faced owing to the Turkish invasions. Gregory planned a new policy. The holy war, so successful in Spain, should be extended into Asia. His friends in Byzantium were in need of military aid. He would gather an army of Christian knights and he would lead it himself to the East. Then, when the infidel had been driven out of Asia Minor, he would hold a Council at Constantinople, where the Christians of the East would compose their differences and gratefully acknowledge the supremacy of Rome.

We do not know if the Emperor knew of or would have welcomed the Papal scheme. He was deposed in 1078. Gregory promptly excommunicated his successor, Nicephorus III; and when Nicephorus was replaced by Alexius Comnenus, he too was excommunicated. The Papal approval was given to the Norman invasion of his territory. Alexius, whose attempts to make friends with the Papacy were rebuffed, turned to ally himself with Gregory's chief enemy, Henry IV of Germany. Meanwhile Gregory himself was caught in the net of disasters woven by his policy and died in exile in 1085, with an anti-Pope reigning in Rome.

Cold though relations now were between Eastern and Western Christendom, there was as yet no official schism. Statesmanship might still preserve the unity of the Church. In Emperor Alexius the East possessed a statesman of the right calibre. A similar statesman now appeared in the West.

Odo de Lagéry was born of a noble family in Champagne in about 1042. He was educated at Rheims and stayed there to become archdeacon, but in 1070 decided to retire to the monastery of Cluny. After a short while he was transferred to Rome, where Gregory VII recognized his ability by making him Cardinal-Bishop of Ostia in 1078. He served for a while as legate in France and in Germany, then returned to be with Gregory in his last unhappy years. He did not approve of Gregory's successor, the weak, unambitious Victor III; but Victor bore him no malice and on his deathbed in September

1087, recommended him to the Cardinals. It was not till March 1088 that a conclave could meet, at Terracina, to elect him Pope as Urban II.

Urban was an impressive man, tall, with a handsome, bearded face and a courteous, persuasive manner. If he lacked Gregory's fire, he was more broad-minded, less obstinate and more skilful in handling men. He could be firm; he had suffered imprisonment in Germany for his loyalty to Gregory. But he preferred to avoid controversy. He came into a difficult heritage. The Normans with whom he had to take refuge were unreliable allies. Elsewhere in Italy Henry IV was in control, with his anti-Pope in Rome. Churches in more distant lands paid little attention to a pontiff so insecurely placed. But, like Alexius, he was a consummate diplomat. Within five years Henry IV had lost his hold on Italy and was facing rebellion in Germany. Urban was installed in Rome. He had brought the Church in France under his control. In Spain his influence was supreme; and the more distant countries of the West accepted his spiritual authority.

He had restored better relations with the East. At a Council at Melfi in 1089 he lifted the ban of excommunication against Alexius. In return he received cordial letters from both the Emperor and the Patriarch of Constantinople; and even the Byzantine theologians who had been eagerly pointing out Roman errors began to adopt a more conciliatory tone.

Early in 1095 Urban summoned representatives of all the Churches of the West to meet him at the first great Council of his reign, to be held in March at Piacenza. There the assembled bishops not only passed decrees against simony, clerical marriage and schism but also discussed the marital misdeeds of the King of France and of Henry IV of Germany. The Council acted as the supreme court of Western Christendom, with the Pope as its presiding judge.

Amongst the visitors attending the Council were ambassadors from the Emperor Alexius. He was ready now to take the offensive against the Turks; but he desperately needed recruits for his army. Here was his opportunity. Urban was sympathetic. The envoys were allowed to address the assembly.

What they actually said is unknown; but it seems that, in order to persuade their audience that it would be meritorious to serve in the Emperor's army, they made an appeal to Christian duty. They emphasized the hardships that the Christians in the East must endure until the infidel was driven back. The bishops must be persuaded that for the safety of Christendom they must send members of their flocks eastward to fight for the faith.

The bishops were impressed, and likewise the Pope. As he journeyed over the Alpine passes into France he turned over in his mind a vaster and more glorious scheme than ever Pope Gregory had envisaged for a holy war in the East.

CHAPTER 5

The summoning

Hearken unto me ye stouthearted, that are far from righteousness.

Isaiah XLVI, 12

Pope Urban arrived in France in the late summer of 1095. On 5 August he was at Valence and on 11 August he reached Le Puy. From there he sent letters to the bishops of France and the neighbouring lands, requesting them to meet him at Clermont in November. Meanwhile he turned south, to spend September in Provence, at Avignon and Saint-Gilles. Early in October he was at Lyons and thence moved on into Burgundy. At Cluny, on 25 October, he consecrated the high altar of the great basilica that Abbot Hugh had begun to build. From Cluny he went to Souvigny, near Moulins, to pay his respects at the tomb of the holiest of Cluniac abbots, Saint Maiolus. The Bishop of Clermont joined him, to escort him to his episcopal city, in readiness for the Council.

As he travelled Urban busied himself with the affairs of the Church in France, organizing and correcting, giving praise and blame where they were due. But his journeyings enabled him also to pursue his further scheme. We do not know whether, while he was in the south, he met in person Raymond of Saint-Gilles, Count of Toulouse and Marquis of Provence, already celebrated for his leadership of the holy wars in Spain. But he was in touch with him and must have heard of his experiences. At Cluny he could talk with men that were concerned with the pilgrim traffic, both to Compostella and to Jerusalem. They could tell him of the overwhelming difficulties that pilgrims to

Palestine had now to endure with the disintegration of Turkish authority there. He learnt that not only were the roads across Asia Minor blocked, but the Holy Land itself was virtually closed to pilgrims.

The Council of Clermont sat from 18 November to 28 November 1095. Some three hundred clerics were present and their work covered a wide range. In general, decrees against lay investiture, simony and clerical marriage were repeated and the Truce of God was advocated. In particular, King Philip was excommunicated for adultery and the Bishop of Cambrai for simony, and the primacy of the see of Lyons over those of Sens and Reims was established. But the Pope wished to use the occasion for a more momentous purpose. It was announced that on Tuesday, 27 November, he would hold a public session, to make a great announcement. The crowds, clerical and lay, that assembled were too huge to be contained within the cathedral, where hitherto the Council had met. The Papal throne was set up on a platform in an open field outside the eastern gate of the city; and when the multitudes were gathered, Urban rose to his feet to address them.

Four contemporary chroniclers have reported the Pope's words for us. One of them, Robert the Monk, claims to have been present at the meeting. Baudri of Dol and Fulcher of Chartres write as though they had been present. The fourth, Guibert of Nogent, probably obtained his version at second hand. But none of them professes to give an accurate verbal account; and each wrote his chronicle a few years later and coloured his account in the light of subsequent events. We can only know approximately what Urban in fact said. It seems that he began his speech by telling his hearers of the necessity for aiding their brethren in the East. Eastern Christendom had appealed for help; for the Turks were advancing into the heart of Christian lands, maltreating the inhabitants and desecrating their shrines. But it was not only of Romania (which is Byzantium) that he spoke. He stressed the special holiness of Jerusalem and described the sufferings of the pilgrims that journeyed there. Having painted the sombre picture, he made his great appeal. Let western Christendom march to the rescue of the East. Rich and poor alike should go. They should leave off slaying each other and fight instead a righteous war, doing the work of God; and God would lead them. For those that died in battle there would be absolution and the remission of sins. Life was miserable and evil here, with men wearing themselves out to the ruin of their bodies and their souls. Here they were poor and unhappy; there they would be joyful and prosperous and true friends of God. There must be no delay. Let them be ready to set out when the summer had come, with God to be their guide.

Urban spoke with fervour and with all the art of a great orator. The response was immediate and tremendous. Cries of 'Deus le volt!' – 'God wills it!' – interrupted the speech. Scarcely had the Pope ended his words before the Bishop of Le Puy rose from his seat and, kneeling before the throne, begged permission to join in the holy expedition. Hundreds crowded up to follow his example. Then the Cardinal Gregory fell on his knees and loudly repeated the *Confiteor*; and all the vast audience echoed it after him. When the prayer was over Urban rose once more and pronounced the absolution and bade his hearers go home.

The enthusiasm was greater than Urban had expected. His plans for its direction were not yet fully made. No great lay lord had been present at Clermont. The recruits were all humbler men. It would be necessary to secure more solid secular support. In the meantime Urban reassembled his bishops for further consultation. The Council had probably already at his request passed a general decree giving remission from temporal penalties for the sins of all that took part with pious intentions in the holy war. It was now added that the worldly belongings of the participants should be placed under the protection of the Church during their absence at the war. The local bishop should be responsible for their safe-keeping and should return them intact when the warrior came home. Each member of the expedition was to wear the sign of the Cross, as a symbol of his dedication; a cross of red material should be sewn on to the shoulder of his surcoat. Anyone that took the Cross should vow to go to Jerusalem. If he turned back too soon or failed to set

out, he would suffer excommunication. Clerics and monks were
not to take the Cross without the permission of their bishop or
abbot. The elderly and infirm must be discouraged from
attempting the expedition; and no one at all should go without
consulting his spiritual adviser. It was not to be a war of mere
conquest. In all towns conquered from the infidel the churches
of the East were to have all their rights and possessions restored
to them. Everyone should be ready to leave his home by the
Feast of the Assumption (15 August) next year, when the
harvests should have been gathered; and the armies should
assemble at Constantinople.

Next, a leader must be appointed. Urban wished to make it
clear that the expedition was under the control of the Church.
Its head must be an ecclesiastic, his legate. With the unanimous
consent of the Council he nominated the Bishop of Le Puy.

Adhemar de Monteil, Bishop of Le Puy, belonged to the
family of the Counts of Valentinois. He was a middle-aged
man, who had already made the pilgrimage to Jerusalem nine
years before. He had earned his leadership by coming forward
as the first to answer Urban's appeal; but as he had already
entertained Urban at Le Puy in August and must have talked
to him there of eastern affairs, it is possible that his stirring
gesture was not entirely spontaneous. It was a wise appointment. Subsequent experience proved him to be a fine
preacher and a tactful diplomat, broad-minded, calm and
kindly, a man whom all would respect but who sought to
persuade rather than to command. His influence was unfail-
ingly used to curb passions and to spread goodwill, but it was
not always firm enough to control the magnates that were
nominally to be under his orders.

The first of the magnates to ask to join the expedition was
Count Raymond of Toulouse. On 1 December, while Urban
was still at Clermont, messengers arrived there to say that the
Count and many of his nobility were eager to take the Cross.
Raymond, who was at Toulouse, could not have heard reports
of the great speech at Clermont. He must have had
forewarning. As the first to be told of the project and the first
to take the vow, he considered that he should be given the

secular leadership over the other great lords. He wished to be Moses to Adhemar's Aaron. Urban would not admit this pretension; but Raymond never entirely abandoned it. In the meantime he planned to cooperate loyally with Adhemar.

Urban left Clermont on 2 December. After visiting various Cluniac houses he spent Christmas at Limoges, where he preached the Crusade in the cathedral, then passed northward through Poitiers to the valley of the Loire. In March he was at Tours, where he held a council; and one Sunday he summoned a congregation to meet him in a meadow by the banks of the river. Standing on an improvised platform he preached a long and solemn sermon, exhorting his hearers to repent and to go on the Crusade. From Tours he turned southward again through Aquitaine, past Saintes and Bordeaux to Toulouse. Toulouse was his headquarters in May and June; and he had many opportunities for discussing the Crusade with his host, Count Raymond. Late in June he moved on to Provence. Raymond accompanied him to Nîmes.

In August the Pope recrossed the Alps into Lombardy. His journey had been no holiday. All the time he was interviewing churchmen and writing letters, seeking to complete his reorganization of the Church in France and, above all, continuing his plans for the Crusade. Synodal letters embodying the decisions taken at Clermont were sent round to the bishops of the West. In some cases provincial councils were held to receive them and to consider local action. It is probable that the chief lay powers were also officially informed of the Pope's desires. From Limoges at the end of 1095 Urban wrote to all the faithful in Flanders referring them to the acts of the Council at Clermont and asking for their support. He had every reason to be satisfied with the response that came from Flanders and the neighbouring lands. In July 1096, while he was at Nîmes, he received a message from King Philip announcing his absolute submission on the matter of his adultery and probably telling at the same time of the adhesion of his brother, Hugh of Vermandois, to the Crusade. During the same month Raymond of Toulouse gave proof of his intentions by handing over many of his possessions to the monastery of Saint-Gilles. It was perhaps on Raymond's advice that Urban decided that the help of a maritime power would be necessary in order to maintain the expedition's supplies. Two legates set out with letters to the republic of Genoa to ask for its cooperation. The republic agreed to provide twelve galleys and a transport, but cautiously delayed their dispatch till it could tell whether the Crusade was a serious movement. It was only in July 1097 that this fleet set sail from Genoa. Meanwhile many Genoese took the Cross.

By the time that Urban was back in Italy he was assured of the success of his scheme. His summons was eagerly obeyed. From as far afield as Scotland, Denmark and Spain, men hastened to make their vows. Some raised money for the journey by pawning their possessions and their lands. Others, expecting never to return, gave everything over to the Church. A sufficient number of great nobles had adhered to the Crusade to give it a formidable military backing. Beside Raymond of Toulouse and Hugh of Vermandois, Robert II of Flanders, Robert, Duke of Normandy, and the latter's brother-in-law Stephen, Count of Blois, were making preparations to set out. More remarkable was the adherence of men devoted to the emperor Henry IV. Chief amongst these was Godfrey of Bouillon, Duke of Lower Lorraine, who took the Cross with his brothers, Eustace, Count of Boulogne, and Baldwin. Grouped round these leaders were many of the lesser nobility and a few eminent ecclesiastics, such as the Bishop of Bayeux.

In Italy Urban found similar enthusiasm. In September 1096 he wrote to the city of Bologna to thank its citizens for their zeal and to caution them not to leave for the East without their priests' permission. Nor should newly married husbands leave without their wives' consent. Meanwhile news of the project had reached southern Italy and was warmly welcomed by many of the Normans there, who were always ready to start on a new adventure. The princes at first held back, but Guiscard's son Bohemond, now prince of Taranto but thwarted in his ambitions in Italy by his brother Roger Borsa and his uncle Roger of Sicily, soon realized the possibilities that the Crusade would open out for him. Together with many of his family and his friends, he took the Cross. Their participation brought to the movement many of the most experienced and enterprising soldiers in Europe. When Urban returned to Rome in time for Christmas 1096, he could feel assured that the Crusade was truly launched.

He had in fact launched a movement greater than he knew. It might have been better if fewer great lords had answered his appeal. For, though with all of them except Bohemond genuine religious fervour was the strongest motive, soon their terrestrial schemes and rivalries would create troubles far beyond the papal legate's control. Still more uncontrollable was the response shown by humbler folk throughout France and Flanders and the Rhineland.

The Pope had asked his bishops to preach the Crusade; but far more effective preaching was done by poorer men, by evangelicals such as Robert of Arbrissel, founder of the Order of Fontevrault, and still more by an itinerant monk called Peter. Peter was an oldish man, born somewhere near Amiens. He had probably tried to make the pilgrimage to Jerusalem a few years previously, but had been maltreated by the Turks and forced to turn back. His contemporaries knew him as Little Peter – *chtou* or *kiokio* in the Picard dialect – but later the hermit's cape that he habitually wore brought him the surname of 'the Hermit', by which he is better known to history. He was a man of short stature, swarthy and with a long, lean face, horribly like the donkey that he always rode and which was revered almost as much as himself. He went barefoot; and his clothes were filthy. He ate neither bread nor meat, but fish, and he drank wine. Despite his lowly appearance he had the power to move men. There was an air of strange authority about him. 'Whatever he said or did', Guibert of Nogent, who knew him personally, tells us, 'it seemed like something half-divine.'

Peter probably had not assisted at the Council of Clermont; but before the year 1095 was out he was already preaching the Crusade. He began his tour in Berry, then moved during February and March through Orléannais and Champagne into Lorraine, and thence past the cities of the Meuse and Aachen to Cologne, where he spent Easter. He gathered

disciples whom he sent to the districts that he could not himself
visit. Among them were the Frenchmen Walter Sans-Avoir,
Rainald of Breis, Geoffrey Burel and Walter of Breteuil, and
the Germans Orel and Gottschalk. Wherever he or his
lieutenants went, men and women left their homes to follow
him. By the time that he reached Cologne his train was
estimated at about 15,000 persons; and many more joined him
in Germany.

The extraordinary success of his preaching was due to many
causes. Life for a peasant in northwestern Europe was grim and
insecure. Much land had gone out of cultivation during the
barbarian invasions and the raids of the Norsemen. Dykes had
been broken, and the sea and rivers had encroached on to the
fields. The lords often opposed the clearing of the forests in
which they hunted for their game. A village unprotected by a
lord's castle was liable to be robbed or burnt by outlaws or by
soldiers fighting petty civil wars. The Church sought to protect
the poor peasants and to establish *bourgs* in empty lands; but its
help was fitful and often unavailing. Greater lords might
encourage the growth of towns, but lesser barons opposed it.
The organization of the demesne was breaking down, but no
orderly system was taking its place. Though actual serfdom had
vanished, men were tied to the land by obligations that they
could not easily escape. Meanwhile the population was
increasing, and holdings in a village could not be subdivided
beyond a certain limit. 'In this land', said Urban at Clermont,
according to Robert the Monk, 'you can scarcely feed the
inhabitants. That is why you use up its goods and excite endless
wars amongst yourselves.' Recent years had been especially
difficult. Floods and pestilence in 1094 had been followed by
drought and a famine in 1095. It was a moment when
emigration seemed very attractive. Already in April 1095 a
shower of meteorites had presaged a great movement of
peoples.

Apocalyptic teaching added to the economic inducement. It
was an age of visions; and Peter was thought to be a visionary.
Medieval man was convinced that the Second Coming was at
hand. He must repent while yet there was time and must go out

to do good. The Church taught that sin could be expiated by pilgrimage and prophecies declared that the Holy Land must be recovered for the faith before Christ could come again. Further, to ignorant minds the distinction between Jerusalem and the New Jerusalem was not very clearly defined. Many of Peter's hearers believed that he was promising to lead them out of their present miseries to the land flowing with milk and honey of which the scriptures spoke. The journey would be hard; there were the legions of Antichrist to be overcome. But the goal was Jerusalem the golden.

What Pope Urban thought of Peter and the success of his preaching no one now knows. His letter to the Bolognese suggests that he was a little nervous of uncontrolled enthusiasm; but he did not, or could not, prevent it from spreading in Italy. Throughout the summer of 1096 a casual but constant stream of pilgrims without leaders or any form of organization began to flow to the East. No doubt he hoped that they and Peter's followers would safely reach Constantinople and there would await the coming of his legate and the military chieftains, who would incorporate them into the orderly ranks of the great Christian army.

Urban's insistence that the expedition should assemble at Constantinople shows how confident he was that the Emperor Alexius would welcome it. Byzantium had asked for soldiers from the West; and here they were answering the summons, not as a few individual mercenaries but in whole powerful armies. His confidence was ingenuous. No government is unwilling to make allies. But when these allies send large armies, over which it has no control, to invade its territory, expecting to be fed and housed and provided with every amenity, then it questions whether the alliance is worth while. When news of the Crusading movement reached Constantinople it aroused feelings of disquiet and alarm.

In 1096 the Byzantine Empire had been enjoying for some months a rare interval of repose. The Emperor had recently defeated a Cuman invasion of the Balkans so decisively that none of the barbarian tribes of the steppes was likely now to attempt to cross the frontier. In Asia Minor, thanks to civil wars encouraged by Byzantine diplomacy, the Seldjuk empire was beginning to disintegrate. Alexius hoped soon to take the offensive against it, but he wished to choose his own time. He still needed a breathing-space in which he could repair his strained resources. The problem of man-power worried him. He wished for mercenaries from the West; and no doubt he hoped that his ambassadors in Italy were successful in their recruitment. Now he was informed that instead of the individual knights or small companies that he expected to join his forces, whole Frankish armies were on the move. He was not pleased, as he knew from experience that the Franks were an unstable race, greedy for money and unscrupulous in keeping agreements. They were formidable in attack; but under the circumstances that was a doubtful advantage. It was with some apprehension that the imperial court learnt, in the words of the Princess Anna Comnena, that 'all the West and all the barbarian tribes from beyond the Adriatic as far as the Pillars of Hercules were moving in a body through Europe towards Asia, bringing whole families with them'. Not only the Emperor but his subjects were uneasy. As a monitory portent great hordes of locusts swept over the Empire, leaving the corn untouched but devouring the vines. Inspired, perhaps, by a hint from the authorities who were anxious not to spread despondency, popular soothsayers interpreted this to mean that the Franks would do no harm to good Christians, whose symbol was the corn, the source of the bread of life, but would destroy the Saracens, a people whose sensuality might well be symbolized by the vine. The Princess Anna was a little sceptical of the interpretation; but the likeness of the Franks to locusts was certainly apparent.

The Emperor Alexius set about calmly making his preparations. The Frankish armies would have to be fed as they travelled through the Empire; and precautions must be taken to keep them from ravaging the countryside and robbing the inhabitants. Stores of provisions were accumulated in each main centre through which they would pass, and a police force was detailed to meet each detachment when it arrived within the Empire and to accompany it to Constantinople. There were

two great roads across the Balkan peninsula, the north road
that crossed the frontier at Belgrade and struck southeast
through Nish, Sofia, Philippopolis and Adrianople, and the Via
Egnatia, from Dyrrhachium through Ochrida and Edessa
(Vodena) to Thessalonica and on through Mosynopolis and
Selymbria to the capital. Since the great German pilgrimage of
1064 the former road had seldom been used by travellers from
the West. The total number of pilgrims had declined and those
that had attempted the journey had preferred the alternative
route. Moreover, Alexius received his information about the
Crusade from Italy. He therefore anticipated that the Frankish
armies would cross the Adriatic and make use of the Via
Egnatia. Supplies were sent to Dyrrhachium and the intervening cities; and the governor of Dyrrhachium, the Emperor's
nephew John Comnenus, was instructed to give the Frankish
leaders a cordial welcome, but to see that they and their armies
were all the time supervised by the military police. High-
ranking envoys from Constantinople would be sent to greet
each leader in turn. Meanwhile the admiral Nicholas
Mavrocatacalon took a flotilla to Adriatic waters to watch the
coasts and give warning of the approach of the Frankish
transports.

The Emperor himself remained at Constantinople, awaiting
further news. Knowing that the Pope had fixed 15 August as
the date of departure for the expedition he did not hurry over
his preparations, when suddenly, at the end of May 1096, a
messenger came posting from the north to say that the first
Frankish army had come down through Hungary and had
entered the Empire at Belgrade.

CHAPTER 6

The people's expedition

The Lord was not able to bring them into the land which
he promised them.

Deuteronomy ix, 28

Peter the hermit arrived with his followers at Cologne on Holy
Saturday, 12 April 1096. There he began to realize the
difficulties that beset the leader of a popular expedition. The
vast motley collection of enthusiasts that he had gathered
together consisted of men from many districts and of many
types. Some brought their women with them, some even their
children. Most of them were peasants, but there were townsfolk
among them, there were junior members of knightly families,
there were former brigands and criminals. Their only link was
the fervour of their faith. All of them had given up everything
to follow Peter; and they were eager to continue on their way.
It was, moreover, essential to keep them on the move if they
were to be fed; for few districts in medieval Europe had a
sufficient surplus of foodstuffs to supply for long the needs of so
large a company. But Cologne was set in a rich countryside
with good river communications. Peter wished to take
advantage of the facilities that it provided to pause a while and
preach to the Germans. He was probably anxious to attract
some of the local nobility to his Crusade. In France and
Flanders the knights preferred to join the company of some
great lord. But no great German lord was going to the holy
war. His preaching was successful. Among the many Germans
that answered his call were several of the lesser nobility, led by
Count Hugh of Tübingen, Count Henry of Schwarzenberg,
Walter of Teck and the three sons of the Count of Zimmern.

But the Frenchmen were impatient. Walter Sans-Avoir decided that he would not wait at Cologne. With a few thousand compatriots he left the city as soon as the Easter Feast was over, probably on Easter Tuesday, and set out on the road to Hungary. Marching up the Rhine and the Neckar and down the Danube, he reached the Hungarian frontier on 8 May. There he sent to King Coloman to ask for permission to cross the kingdom and for help in obtaining provisions for his men. Coloman proved friendly. The army passed through Hungary without an untoward incident. About the end of the month it reached Semlin on the further frontier, and crossed the River Save into Byzantine territory at Belgrade.

The military commander at Belgrade was taken by surprise. He had received no instructions on how to deal with such an invasion. He sent posthaste to Nish, where the governor of the Bulgarian province resided, to inform him of Walter's arrival. The governor, a conscientious but undistinguished official called Nicetas, was equally uninstructed. In his turn he dispatched a messenger to take the news as quickly as possible to Constantinople. Meanwhile Walter at Belgrade demanded food for his followers. The harvests were not yet gathered, and the garrison had none to spare; so Walter and his troops began to pillage the countryside. His temper was inflamed owing to an unfortunate occurrence at Semlin, where sixteen of his men, who had not crossed the river with their companions, tried to rob a bazaar. The Hungarians captured them and stripped them of their arms and their clothing, which were hung on the walls of Semlin as a warning, and sent them on naked across to Belgrade. When the pillaging around Belgrade began the commander resorted to arms. In the fighting several of Walter's men were killed and others were burnt alive in a church.

Walter was eventually able to march on to Nish, where Nicetas received him kindly and provided food, keeping him there till he received an answer from Constantinople. The Emperor, who had believed that the Crusade would not leave the West before the Feast of the Assumption, was forced to speed up his arrangements. Nicetas was requested to send Walter on under escort. Accompanied by this escort Walter and his army continued their journey in peace. Early in July they reached Philippopolis, where Walter's uncle, Walter of Poissy, died; and by the middle of the month they were in Constantinople.

From Walter Nicetas must have learnt that Peter was not far behind, with a far larger company. He therefore moved up to Belgrade to meet him and made contact with the Hungarian governor of Semlin.

Peter left Cologne on about 20 April. The Germans at first had mocked at his preaching; but by now many thousands had joined him, till his followers probably numbered close on 20,000 men and women. Other Germans, fired by his enthusiasm, planned to follow later, under Gottschalk and Count Emich of Leisingen. From Cologne Peter took the usual road up the Rhine and the Neckar to the Danube. When they reached the Danube, some of his company decided to travel by boat down the river; but Peter and his main body marched by the road running south of Lake Ferto and entered Hungary at Oedenburg. Peter himself rode on his donkey, and the German knights on horseback, while lumbering wagons carried such stores as he possessed and the chest of money that he had collected for the journey. But the vast majority travelled on foot. Where the roads were good they managed to cover twenty-five miles a day.

King Coloman received Peter's emissaries with the same benevolence that he had shown to Walter, warning them only that any attempt to pillage would be punished. The army moved peaceably through Hungary during late May and early June. At some point, probably near Karlovci, it was rejoined by the detachments that had travelled by boat. On 20 June it reached Semlin.

There its troubles began. What actually happened is obscure. It seems that the governor, who was a Ghuzz Turk in origin, was alarmed by the size of the army. Together with his colleague across the frontier he attempted to tighten up police regulations. Peter's army was suspicious. It heard rumours of the sufferings of Walter's men; it feared that the two governors were plotting against it; and it was shocked by the sight of the arms of Walter's sixteen miscreants still hanging on the city walls. But all might have been well had not a dispute arisen over the sale of a pair of shoes. This led to a riot, which turned into a pitched battle. Probably against Peter's wishes, his men, led by Geoffrey Burel, attacked the town and succeeded in storming the citadel. Four thousand Hungarians were killed and a large store of provisions captured. Then, terrified of the vengeance of the Hungarian king, they made all haste to cross the river Save.

They took all the wood that they could collect from the houses, with which to build themselves rafts. Nicetas, watching anxiously from Belgrade, tried to control the crossing of the river, and to oblige them to use one ford only. His troops were mainly composed of Petcheneg mercenaries, men that could be trusted to obey his orders blindly. They were sent in barges to prevent any crossing except at the proper place. He himself, recognizing that he had insufficient troops for dealing with such a horde, retired back to Nish, where the military headquarters of the province were placed. On his departure the inhabitants of Belgrade deserted the town and took to the mountains.

On 26 June Peter's army forced its way across the Save. When the Petchenegs tried to restrict them to one passage, they were attacked. Several of the boats were sunk and the soldiers aboard captured and put to death. The army entered Belgrade and set fire to it, after a wholesale pillage. Then it marched on for seven days through the forests and arrived at Nish on 3 July. Peter sent at once to Nicetas to ask for supplies of food.

Nicetas had informed Constantinople of Peter's approach, and was awaiting the officials and military escort that were coming to convoy the westerners on to the capital. He had a large garrison at Nish; and he had strengthened it by recruiting locally additional Petcheneg and Hungarian mercenaries. But he probably could not spare any men to act as Peter's escort until the troops from Constantinople should meet him. On the other hand it was impracticable and dangerous to allow so vast a company to linger long at Nish. Peter was requested therefore to provide hostages while food was collected for his men and then to move on as soon as possible. All went well at first. Geoffrey Burel and Walter of Breteuil were handed over as hostages. The local inhabitants not only allowed the Crusaders to acquire the supplies that they needed, but many of them gave alms to the poorer pilgrims. Some even asked to join the pilgrimage.

Next morning the Crusaders started out along the road to Sofia. As they were leaving the town some Germans who had quarrelled with a townsman on the previous night wantonly set fire to a group of mills by the river. Hearing of this, Nicetas sent troops to attack the rearguard and to take some prisoners whom he could hold as hostages. Peter was riding his donkey about a mile ahead and knew nothing of all this till a man called Lambert ran up from the rear to tell him. He hurried back to interview Nicetas and to arrange for the ransom of the captives. But while they were conferring, rumours of fighting and of treachery spread round the army. A company of hotheads thereupon turned and assailed the fortifications of the town. The garrison drove them off and counter-attacked; then while Peter, who had gone to restrain his men, tried to re-establish contact with Nicetas, another group insisted upon renewing the attack. Nicetas therefore let all his forces loose on the Crusaders, who were completely routed and scattered. Many of them were slain; many were captured, men, women and children, and spent the rest of their days in captivity in the neighbourhood. Amongst other things Peter lost his money-chest. Peter himself, with Rainald of Breis and Walter of Breteuil and about five hundred men, fled up a mountainside, believing that they alone survived. But next morning seven thousand others caught them up; and they continued on the road. At the deserted town of Bela Palanka they paused to gather the local harvest, as they had no food left. There many more stragglers joined them. When they continued on their march they found that a quarter of their company had been lost.

They reached Sofia on 12 July. There they met the envoys and the escort, sent from Constantinople with orders to keep them fully supplied and to see that they never delayed anywhere for more than three days. Thenceforward their journey passed smoothly. The local population was friendly. At

Philippopolis the Greeks were so deeply moved by the stories of their suffering that they freely gave them money, horses and mules. Two days outside Adrianople more envoys greeted Peter with a gracious message from the Emperor. It was decided that the expedition should be forgiven for its crimes, as it had been already sufficiently punished. Peter wept with joy at the favour shown him by so great a potentate.

The Emperor's kindly interest did not cease when the Crusaders arrived at Constantinople on 1 August. He was curious to see its leader; and Peter was summoned to an audience at the court, where he was given money and good advice. To Alexius's experienced eye the expedition was not impressive. He feared that if it crossed into Asia it would soon be destroyed by the Turks. But its indiscipline obliged him to move it as soon as possible from the neighbourhood of Constantinople. The westerners committed endless thefts. They broke into the palaces and villas in the suburbs; they even stole the lead from the roofs of churches. Though their entry into Constantinople itself was strictly controlled, only small parties of sightseers being admitted through the gates, it was impossible to police the whole neighbourhood.

Walter Sans-Avoir and his men were already at Constantinople, and various bands of Italian pilgrims arrived there about the same time. They joined up with Peter's expedition; and on 6 August the whole of his forces were conveyed across the Bosphorus. From the Asiatic shore they marched in an unruly manner, pillaging houses and churches, along the coast of the Sea of Marmora to Nicomedia, which lay deserted since its sack by the Turks fifteen years before. There a quarrel broke out between the Germans and the Italians on the one side and the French on the other. The former broke away from Peter's command and elected as their leader an Italian lord called Rainald. At Nicomedia the two parts of the army turned westward along the south coast of the Gulf of Nicomedia to a fortified camp called Cibotos by the Greeks and Civetot by the Crusaders, which Alexius had prepared for the use of his own English mercenaries in the neighbourhood of Helenopolis. It was a convenient camping-ground, as the district was fertile and further supplies could easily be brought by sea from Constantinople.

Alexius had urged Peter to await the coming of the main Crusading armies before attempting any attack on the infidel; and Peter was impressed by his advice. But Peter's authority was waning. Both the Germans and Italians, under Rainald, and his own Frenchmen, over whom Geoffrey Burel seems to have held the chief influence, instead of quietly recuperating their strength, vied with each other in raiding the countryside. First they pillaged the immediate neighbourhood; then they cautiously advanced into territory held by the Turks, making forays and robbing the villagers, who were all Christian Greeks. In the middle of September several thousand of the Frenchmen ventured as far as the gates of Nicaea, the capital of the Seldjuk Sultan, Kilij Arslan ibn-Suleiman. They sacked the villages in the suburbs, rounding up the flocks and herds that they found and torturing and massacring the Christian inhabitants with horrifying savagery. It was said that they roasted babies on spits. A Turkish detachment sent out from the city was driven off after a fierce combat. They then returned to Civetot, where they sold their booty to their comrades and to the Greek sailors who were about the camp.

This profitable French raid roused the jealousy of the Germans. Towards the end of September Rainald set out with a German expedition of some six thousand men, including priests and even bishops. They marched beyond Nicaea, pillaging as they went, but, kinder than the Frenchmen, sparing the Christians, till they came to a castle called Xerigordon. This they managed to capture; and, finding it well stocked with provisions of every sort, they planned to make it a centre from which they could raid the countryside. On hearing of the Crusaders exploit, the Sultan sent a high military commander with a large force to recapture the castle. Xerigordon was set on a hill, and its water supply came from a well just outside the walls and a spring in the valley below. The Turkish army, arriving before the castle on St Michael's Day, 29 September, defeated an ambush laid by Rainald and, taking possession of the spring and the well, kept the Germans

closely invested within the castle. Soon the besieged grew
desperate from thirst. They tried to suck moisture from the
earth; they cut the veins of their horses and donkeys to drink
their blood; they even drank each other's urine. Their priests
tried vainly to comfort and encourage them. After eight days of
agony Rainald decided to surrender. He opened the gates to
the enemy on receiving a promise that his life would be spared
if he renounced Christianity. Everyone that remained true to
the faith was slaughtered. Rainald and those that apostasized
with him were sent into captivity, to Antioch and to Aleppo
and far into Khorassan.

News of the capture of Xerigordon by the Germans had
reached the camp at Civetot early in October. It was followed
by a rumour, spread by two Turkish spies, that they had taken
Nicaea itself and were dividing up the booty for their benefit.
As the Turks expected, this caused tumultuous excitement in
the camp. The soldiers clamoured to be allowed to hasten to
Nicaea, along roads that the Sultan had carefully ambushed.
Their leaders had difficulty in restraining them, till suddenly
the truth was discovered about the fate of Rainald's expedition.
The excitement was changed to panic; and the chiefs of the
army met to discuss what next to do. Peter had gone to
Constantinople. His authority over the army had vanished. He
hoped to revive it by obtaining some important material aid
from the Emperor. There was a movement in the army to go
out to avenge Xerigordon. But Walter Sans-Avoir persuaded
his colleagues to await Peter's return, which was due in eight
days' time. Peter, however, did not return; and meanwhile it
was reported that the Turks were approaching in force towards
Civetot. The army council met again. The more responsible
leaders, Walter Sans-Avoir, Rainald of Breis, Walter of Breteuil
and Fulk of Orleans, and the Germans, Hugh of Tübingen and
Walter of Teck, still urged that nothing should be done till
Peter arrived. But Geoffrey Burel, with the public opinion of
the army behind him, insisted that it would be cowardly and
foolish not to advance against the enemy. He had his way. On
21 October, at dawn, the whole army of the Crusaders,
numbering over 20,000 men, marched out from Civetot,

leaving behind them only old men, women and children and the sick.

Barely three miles from the camp, where the road to Nicaea entered a narrow wooded valley, by a village called Dracon, the Turks were lying in ambush. The Crusaders marched noisily and carelessly, the knights on horseback at their head. Suddenly a hail of arrows from the woods killed or maimed the horses; and as they plunged in confusion, unseating their riders, the Turks attacked. The cavalry, pursued by the Turks, was flung back on to the infantry. Many of the knights fought bravely, but they could not stop the panic that seized the army. In a few minutes the whole host was fleeing in utter disorder to Civetot. There in the camp the daily round was just beginning. Some of the older folk were still asleep in their beds. Here and there a priest was celebrating early mass. Into its midst there burst a horde of terrified fugitives with the enemy on their heels. There was no real resistance. Soldiers, women and priests were massacred before they had time to move. Some fled into the forests around, others into the sea, but few of them escaped for long. Others defended themselves for a while by lighting bonfires which the wind blew into the Turks' faces. Only young boys and girls whose appearance pleased the Turks were spared, together with a few captives made after the first heat of the fighting was over. These were taken away into slavery. Some three thousand, luckier than the rest, managed to reach an old castle that stood by the sea. It had long been out of use, and its doors and windows were dismantled. But the refugees, with the energy of despair, improvised fortifications from the wood that lay about and reinforced them with bones, and were able to beat off the attacks of the enemy.

The castle held out; but elsewhere on the field by midday all was over. Corpses covered the ground from the pass of Dracon to the sea. Amongst the dead were Walter Sans-Avoir, Rainald of Breis, Fulk of Orleans, Hugh of Tübingen, Walter of Teck, Conrad and Albert of Zimmern and many other of the German knights. The only leaders to survive were Geoffrey Burel, whose impetuousness had caused the disaster, Walter of Breteuil and William of Poissy, Henry of Schwarzenberg, Frederick of

Zimmern and Rudolf of Brandis, almost all of whom were
badly wounded.

When dusk fell a Greek who was with the army succeeded in
finding a boat and set sail for Constantinople, to tell Peter and
the Emperor of the battle. Of Peter's feelings we have no
record; but Alexius at once ordered some men-of-war, with
strong forces aboard, to sail for Civetot. On the arrival of the
Byzantine battle-squadron the Turks raised the siege of the
castle and retired inland. The survivors were taken off to the
ships and returned to Constantinople. There they were given
quarters in the suburbs;, but their arms were removed from
them.

The People's Crusade was over. It had cost many thousands
of lives; it had tried the patience of the Emperor and his
subjects; and it had taught that faith alone, without wisdom
and discipline, would not open the road to Jerusalem.

CHAPTER 7

The German crusade

Ah Lord God! wilt thou destroy all the residue of Israel?

Ezekiel IX, 8

Peter the hermit's departure for the East had not ended Crusading enthusiasm in Germany. He had left behind him his disciple Gottschalk to collect a further army; and many other preachers and leaders prepared to follow his example. But, though the Germans responded in thousands to the appeal, they were less eager than the French had been to hurry to the Holy Land. There was work to be done first nearer home.

Jewish colonies had been established for centuries past along the trade routes of western Europe. Their inhabitants were Sephardic Jews, whose ancestors had spread out from the Mediterranean basin throughout the Dark Ages. They kept up connections with their co-religionists in Byzantium and in Arab lands, and were thus enabled to play a large part in international trade, more especially the trade between Moslem and Christian countries. The prohibition of usury in western Christian countries and its strict control in Byzantium left them an open field for the establishment of money-lending houses throughout Christendom. Their technical skill and long traditions made them pre-eminent also in the practice of medicine. Except long ago in Visigothic Spain they had never undergone serious persecution in the West. They had no civic rights; but both lay and ecclesiastical authorities were pleased to give special protection to such useful members of the community. The kings of France and Germany had always befriended them; and they were shown particular favour by the archbishops of the great cities of the Rhineland. But the peasants and poorer townsmen, increasingly in need of money as a cash economy replaced the older economy of services, fell more and more into their debt and in consequence felt more and more resentment against them; while the Jews, lacking legal security, charged high rates of interest and extracted exorbitant profits wherever the benevolence of the local ruler supported them.

Their unpopularity grew throughout the eleventh century, as more classes of the community began to borrow money from them; and the beginnings of the Crusading movement added to it. It was expensive for a knight to equip himself for a Crusade; if he had no land and no possessions to pledge, he must borrow money from the Jews. But was it right that in order to go and fight for Christendom he must fall into the clutches of members of the race that crucified Christ? The poorer Crusader was often already in debt to the Jews. Was it right that he should be hampered in his Christian duty by obligations to one of the impious race? The evangelical preaching of the Crusade laid stress on Jerusalem, the scene of the Crucifixion. It inevitably drew attention to the people at whose hands Christ had suffered. The Moslems were the present enemy; they were persecuting Christ's followers. But the Jews were surely worse; they had persecuted Christ Himself.

Already in the Spanish wars there had been some inclination on the part of Christian armies to maltreat the Jews. At the time of the expedition to Barbastro Pope Alexander II wrote to the bishops in Spain to remind them that there was all the difference in the world between the Moslems and the Jews. The former were irreconcilable enemies to the Christians, but the latter were ready to work for them. But in Spain the Jews had enjoyed such favour from the hands of the Moslems that the Christian conquerors could not bring themselves to trust them.

In December 1095 the Jewish communities of northern France wrote to their co-religionists in Germany to warn them that the Crusading movement was likely to cause trouble to their race. There were reports of a massacre of the Jews at Rouen. It is unlikely that such a massacre in fact occurred; but the Jews were sufficiently alarmed for Peter the Hermit to bring off a successful stroke of business. Hinting, no doubt, that otherwise he might find it difficult to restrain his followers, he obtained from the French Jews letters of introduction to the Jewish communities throughout Europe, calling upon them to welcome him and to supply him and his army with all the provisions that he might require.

About the same time Godfrey of Bouillon, Duke of Lower Lorraine, began his preparations to start out on the Crusade. A rumour ran round the province that he had vowed before he left to avenge the death of Christ with the blood of the Jews. In terror the Jews of the Rhineland induced Kalonymos, chief Rabbi of Mainz, to write to Godfrey's overlord, the emperor Henry IV, who had always shown himself a friend to their race, to urge him to forbid the persecution. At the same time, to be on the safe side, the Jewish communities of Mainz and Cologne each offered the Duke the sum of five hundred pieces of silver. Henry wrote to his chief vassals, lay and ecclesiastic, to bid them guarantee the safety of all the Jews on their lands. Godfrey, having already succeeded in his blackmail, answered that nothing was further from his thoughts than persecution, and gladly gave the requested guarantee.

If the Jews hoped to escape so cheaply from the threat of Christian fervour, they were soon to be disillusioned. At the end of April 1096, a certain Volkmar, of whose origins we know nothing, set out from the Rhineland with over ten thousand men to join Peter in the East. He took the road to Hungary that ran through Bohemia. A few days later Peter's old disciple Gottschalk, with a slightly larger company, left along the main road that Peter had taken, up the Rhine and through Bavaria. Meanwhile a third army had been collected by a petty lord of the Rhineland, Count Emich of Leisingen, who had already acquired a certain reputation for lawlessness and brigandage. Emich now claimed to have a cross miraculously branded on his flesh. At the same time, as a soldier of known experience, he attracted to his banner a greater and more formidable variety of recruits than the preachers Volkmar and Gottschalk could command. A multitude of simple enthusiastic pilgrims joined him, some of them following a goose that had been inspired by God. But his army included members of the French and German nobility, such as the lords of Zweibrücken, Salm and

Viernenberger, Hartmann of Dillingen, Drogo of Nesle, Clarambald of Vendeuil, Thomas of La Fère and William, Viscount of Melun, surnamed the Carpenter because of his huge physical strength.

It was perhaps the example of Peter and of Duke Godfrey that suggested to Emich how easily religious fervour could be used to the personal profit of himself and his associates. Ignoring the special orders of the emperor Henry, he persuaded his followers to begin their Crusade on 3 May with an attack on the Jewish community at Spier, close to his home. It was not a very impressive attack. The Bishop of Spier, whose sympathies were won by a handsome present, placed the Jews under his protection. Only twelve were taken by the Crusaders and slain after their refusal to embrace Christianity; and one Jewess committed suicide to preserve her virtue. The bishop saved the rest and even managed to capture several of the murderers, whose hands were cut off in punishment.

Small as was the massacre at Spier, it whetted the appetite. On 18 May Emich and his troops arrived at Worms. Soon afterwards a rumour went round that the Jews had taken a Christian and drowned him and used the water in which they had kept his corpse to poison the city wells. The Jews were not popular at Worms nor in the countryside around; and the rumour brought townsfolk and peasants to join with Emich's men in attacks on the Jewish quarter. Every Jew that was captured was put to death. As at Spier the bishop intervened and opened his palace to Jewish refugees. But Emich and the angry crowds with him forced the gates and broke into the sanctuary. There, despite the bishop's protests, they slaughtered all his guests, to the number of about five hundred.

The massacre at Worms took place on 20 May. On 25 May Emich arrived before the great city of Mainz. He found the gates closed against him by order of Archbishop Rothard. But the news of his coming provoked anti-Jewish riots within the city, in the course of which a Christian was killed. So on 26 May friends within the city opened the gates to him. The Jews, who had assembled at the synagogue, sent gifts of two hundred marks of silver to the archbishop and to the chief lay lord of the city, asking to be taken into their respective palaces. At the same time a Jewish emissary went to Emich and for seven gold pounds bought from him a promise that he would spare the community. The money was wasted. Next day he attacked the archbishop's palace. Rothard, alarmed by the temper of the assailants, hastened to flee with all his staff. On his departure Emich's men broke into the building. The Jews attempted to resist but were soon overcome and slain. Their lay protector, whose name has not survived, may have been more courageous. But Emich succeeded in setting fire to his palace and forced its inmates to evacuate it. Several Jews saved their lives by abjuring their faith. The remainder were killed. The massacre lasted for two more days, while refugees were rounded up. Some of the apostates repented of their weakness and committed suicide. One, before slaying himself and his family, burnt down the synagogue to keep it from further desecration. The chief Rabbi, Kalonymos, with about fifty companions, had escaped from the city to Rüdesheim and begged asylum from the archbishop who was staying at his country villa there. To the archbishop, seeing the terror of his visitors, it seemed a propitious moment to attempt their conversion. This was more than Kalonymos could bear. He snatched up a knife and flung himself on his host. He was beaten off; but the outrage cost him and his comrades their lives. In the course of the massacre at Mainz about a thousand Jews had perished.

Emich next proceeded towards Cologne. There had already been anti-Jewish riots there in April; and now the Jews, panic-stricken by the news from Mainz, scattered themselves among the neighbouring villages and the houses of their Christian acquaintances, who kept them hidden over Whit Sunday, 1 June, and the following day, while Emich was in the neighbourhood. The synagogue was burnt and a Jew and a Jewess who refused to apostasize were slain; but the arch-bishop's influence was able to prevent further excesses.

At Cologne Emich decided that his work in the Rhineland was completed. Early in June he set out with the bulk of his forces up the Main towards Hungary. But a large party of his followers thought that the Moselle valley also should be purged of Jews. They broke off from his army at Mainz and on 1 June they arrived at Trier. Most of the Jewish community there was safely given refuge by the archbishop in his palace; but as the Crusaders approached some Jews in panic began to fight among themselves, while others threw themselves into the Moselle and were drowned. Their persecutors then moved on to Metz, where twenty-two Jews perished. About the middle of June they returned to Cologne, hoping to rejoin Emich; but, finding him gone, they proceeded down the Rhine, spending from 24 to 27 June in massacring the Jews at Neuss, Wevelinghofen, Eller and Xanten. Then they dispersed, some returning home, others probably merging with the army of Godfrey of Bouillon.

News of Emich's exploits reached the parties that had already left Germany for the East. Volkmar and his followers arrived at Prague at the end of May. On 30 June they began to massacre the Jews in the city. The lay authorities were unable to curb them; and the vehement protests of Bishop Cosmas were unheeded. From Prague Volkmar marched on into Hungary. At Nitra, the first large town across the frontier, he probably attempted to take similar action. But the Hungarians would not permit such behaviour. Finding the Crusaders incorrigibly unruly they attacked and scattered them. Many were slain and others captured. What happened to the survivors and to Volkmar himself is unknown.

Gottschalk and his men, who had taken the road through Bavaria, had paused at Ratisbon to massacre the Jews there. A few days later they entered Hungary at Wiesselburg (Moson). King Coloman issued orders that they should be given facilities for revictualling so long as they behaved themselves. But from the outset they began to pillage the countryside, stealing wine and corn and sheep and oxen. The Hungarian peasants resisted these exactions. There was fighting; several deaths occurred and a young Hungarian boy was impaled by the Crusaders. Coloman brought up troops to control them and surrounded them at the village of Stuhlweissenburg, a little further to the east. The Crusaders were obliged to surrender all their arms and all the goods that they had stolen. But trouble continued. Possibly they made some attempt to resist; possibly Coloman had heard by now of the events at Nitra and would not trust them even disarmed. As they lay at its mercy, the Hungarian army fell on them. Gottschalk was the first to flee but was soon taken. All his men perished in the massacre.

Some few weeks later Emich's army approached the Hungarian frontier. It was larger and more formidable than Gottschalk's; and King Coloman, after his recent experiences, was seriously alarmed. When Emich sent to ask for permission to pass through his kingdom, Coloman refused the request and sent troops to defend the bridge that led across a branch of the Danube to Wiesselburg. But Emich was not to be deflected. For six weeks his men fought the Hungarians in a series of petty skirmishes in front of the bridge, while they set about building an alternative bridge for themselves. In the meantime they pillaged the country on their side of the river. At last the Crusaders were able to force their way across the bridge that they had built and laid siege to the fortress of Wiesselburg itself. Their army was well equipped and possessed siege-engines of such power that the fall of the town seemed imminent. But, probably on the rumour that the king was coming up in full strength, a sudden panic flung the Crusaders into disorder. The garrison thereupon made a sortie and fell on the Crusaders' camp. Emich was unable to rally his men. After a short battle they were utterly routed. Most of them fell on the field; but Emich himself and a few knights were able to escape owing to the speed of their horses. Emich and his German companions eventually retired to their homes. The French knights, Clarambald of Vendeuil, Thomas of La Fère and William the Carpenter, joined other expeditions bound for Palestine.

The collapse of Emich's Crusade, following so soon after the collapse of Volkmar's and Gottschalk's Crusades, deeply impressed western Christendom. To most good Christians it appeared as a punishment meted out from on high to the murderers of the Jews. Others, who had thought the whole Crusading movement to be foolish and wrong, saw in these disasters God's open disavowal of it all. Nothing had yet occurred to justify the cry that echoed at Clermont, 'Deus le volt'.

CHAPTER 8

The Princes and the Emperor

Will he make many supplications unto thee? will he speak
soft words unto thee? Will he make a covenant with thee?

Job XLI, 3, 4

The western princes that had taken the Cross were less
impatient than Peter and his friends. They were ready to abide
by the Pope's time-table. Their troops had to be gathered and
equipped. Money had to be raised for the purpose. They must
arrange for the government of their lands during an absence
that might last for years. None of them was prepared to start
out before the end of August.

The first to leave his home was Hugh, Count of Vermandois,
known as Le Maisné, the younger, a surname translated most
inappropriately by the Latin chroniclers even in his own time
as Magnus. He was the younger son of King Henry I of France
and of a princess of Scandinavian origin, Anne of Kiev; a man
of some forty years of age, of greater rank than wealth, who had
acquired his small county by marriage with its heiress, and had
never played a prominent part in French politics. He was
proud of his lineage but ineffectual in action. We cannot tell
what were his motives in joining the Crusade. No doubt he
inherited the restlessness of his Scandinavian ancestors. Perhaps
he felt that in the East he could acquire the power and riches
that befitted his high birth. Probably his brother, King Philip,
encouraged his decision in order to ingratiate his family with
the Papacy. Leaving his lands in the care of his countess, he set
out in late August for Italy, with a small army composed of his
vassals and some knights from his brother's domains. Before his

departure he sent a special messenger ahead of him to Constantinople, requesting the Emperor to arrange for his reception with the honours due to a prince of royal blood. As he journeyed southward he was joined by Drogo of Nesle and Clarambald of Vendeuil and William the Carpenter and other French knights returning from Emich's disastrous expedition.

Hugh and his company passed by Rome and arrived at Bari early in October. In southern Italy they found the Norman princes themselves preparing for the Crusade; and Bohemond's nephew William decided not to wait for his relatives but to cross the sea with Hugh. From Bari Hugh sent an embassy of twenty-four knights, led by William the Carpenter, across to Dyrrhachium to inform the governor that he was about to arrive and to repeat his demand for a suitable reception. The governor, John Comnenus, was thus able to warn the Emperor of his approach and himself prepared to welcome him. But Hugh's actual arrival was not as dignified as he had hoped. A storm wrecked the small flotilla that he had hired for the crossing. Some of his ships foundered with all their passengers. Hugh himself was cast ashore on Cape Palli, a few miles to the north of Dyrrhachium. John's envoys found him there bewildered and bedraggled, and escorted him to their master; who at once re-equipped him and feasted him and showed him every attention, but kept him under strict surveillance. Hugh was pleased with the flattering regard shown to him; but to some of his followers it seemed that he was being kept a prisoner. He remained at Dyrrhachium till a high official, the admiral Manuel Butumites, arrived from the Emperor to escort him to Constantinople. His journey thither was achieved in comfort, though he was obliged to take a roundabout route through Philippopolis, as the Emperor did not wish to let him make contact with the Italian pilgrims that were crowding along the Via Egnatia. At Constantinople Alexius greeted him warmly and showered presents on him but continued to restrict his liberty.

Hugh's arrival forced Alexius to declare his policy towards the western princes. The information that he had acquired and his memory of the career of Roussel of Bailleul convinced him that, whatever might be the official reasons for the Crusade, the real object of the Franks was to secure for themselves principalities in the East. He did not object to this. So long as the Empire recovered all the lands that it had held before the Turkish invasions, there was much to be said in favour of the creation of Christian bufferstates on its perimeter. That small states could be independent was unthought-of at the time. But Alexius wished to be sure that he would be clearly regarded as overlord of any that might be erected. Knowing that in the West allegiance was established by a solemn oath, he decided to demand such an oath from all the western leaders to cover their future conquests. To win their compliance he was ready to pour gifts and subsidies on them, while he would emphasize his own wealth and glory, that they might not feel their dignity lowered in becoming his men. Hugh, dazzled by the magnificence and the generosity of the Emperor, fell in willingly with his plans. But the next to arrive from the West was not so easily persuaded.

Godfrey of Bouillon, Duke of Lower Lorraine, appears in later legend as the perfect Christian knight, the peerless hero of the whole Crusading epic. A scrupulous study of history must modify the verdict. He was born about the year 1060, the second son of Count Eustace II of Boulogne and of Ida, daughter of Godfrey II, Duke of Lower Lorraine, who was descended in the female line from Charlemagne. He had been designated as the heir to the possessions of his mother's family; but on her father's death the emperor Henry IV confiscated the duchy, leaving Godfrey only the county of Antwerp and the lordship of Bouillon in the Ardennes. Godfrey, however, served Henry so loyally in his German and Italian campaigns that in 1082 he was invested with the duchy, but as an office, not as a hereditary fief. Lorraine was impregnated with Cluniac influences; and, though Godfrey remained loyal to the emperor, it is possible that Cluniac teaching, with its strong papal sympathies, began to trouble his conscience. His administration of Lorraine was not very efficient. There seems to have been some doubt whether Henry would continue to employ him. It was therefore partly from despondency about his future in Lorraine, partly from uneasiness over his religious loyalties, and partly from genuine enthusiasm that he answered the call to the Crusade. He made his preparations very thoroughly. After raising money by blackmailing the Jews, he sold his estates of Rosay and Stenay on the Meuse, and pledged his castle of Bouillon to the Bishop of Liège, and was thus able to equip an army of considerable size. The number of his troops and his former high office gave Godfrey a prestige that was enhanced by his pleasant manners and his handsome appearance. For he was tall, well-built and fair, with a yellow beard and hair, the ideal picture of a northern knight. But he was indifferent as a soldier, and as a personality he was overshadowed by his younger brother, Baldwin.

Godfrey's two brothers had also taken the Cross. The elder, Eustace III, Count of Boulogne, was an unenthusiastic Crusader, always eager to return to his rich lands that lay on both sides of the English Channel. His contribution of soldiers was far smaller than Godfrey's, whom he was therefore content to regard as leader. He probably travelled out separately, going through Italy. The younger brother, Baldwin, who accompanied Godfrey, was of a different type. He had been destined for the Church and so had not been allotted any of the family estates. But, though his training at the great school at Reims left him with a lasting taste for culture, his temperament was not that of a churchman. He returned to lay life and apparently took service under his brother Godfrey in Lorraine. The brothers formed a striking contrast. Baldwin was even taller than Godfrey. His hair was as dark as the other's was fair; but his skin was very white. While Godfrey was gracious in manner, Baldwin was haughty and cold. Godfrey's tastes were simple, but Baldwin though he could endure great hardships, loved pomp and luxury. Godfrey's private life was chaste, Baldwin's given over to venery. Baldwin welcomed the Crusade with delight. His homeland offered him no future; but in the East he might find himself a kingdom. When he set out he took with him his Norman wife, Godvere of Tosni, and their little children. He did not intend to return.

Godfrey and his brothers were joined by many leading

knights from Walloon and Lotharingian territory; their cousin, Baldwin of Rethel, lord of Le Bourg, Baldwin II, Count of Hainault, Rainald, Count of Toul, Warner of Gray, Dudo of Konz-Saarburg, Baldwin of Stavelot, Peter of Stenay and the brothers Henry and Geoffrey of Esch.

Perhaps because he felt some embarrassment as an imperialist in his relations with the Papacy, Godfrey decided not to travel through Italy by the route that the other crusading leaders were planning to take. Instead, he would go through Hungary, following not only the Popular Crusades but also, according to the legend that was now spreading through the West, his ancestor Charlemagne himself on his pilgrimage to Jerusalem. He left Lorraine at the end of August, and after a few weeks' marching up the Rhine and down the Danube he arrived at the beginning of October at the Hungarian frontier on the river Leitha. From there he sent an embassy, headed by Geoffrey of Esch, who had previous experience of the Hungarian court, to King Coloman to ask for permission to cross his territory.

Coloman had recently suffered too severely at the hands of Crusaders to welcome a new invasion. He kept the embassy for eight days, then announced that he would meet Godfrey at Oedenburg for an interview. Godfrey came with a few of his knights and was invited to spend some days at the Hungarian Court. The impression that Coloman received from this visit decided him to allow the passage of Godfrey's army through Hungary, provided that Baldwin, whom he guessed to be its most dangerous member, was left with him as a hostage, together with his wife and children. When Godfrey returned to his army, Baldwin at first refused to give himself up; but he later consented; and Godfrey and his troops entered the kingdom at Oedenburg. Coloman promised to provide them with provisions at reasonable prices; while Godfrey sent heralds round his army to announce that any act of violence would be punished by death. After these precautions had been taken the Crusaders marched peaceably through Hungary, the king and his army keeping close watch on them all the way. After spending three days revictualling at Mangjeloz, close to the

Byzantine frontier, Godfrey reached Semlin towards the end of November and took his troops in an orderly manner across the Save to Belgrade. As soon as they were all across, the hostages were returned to him.

The imperial authorities, probably forewarned by the Hungarians, were ready to welcome him. Belgrade itself had lain deserted since its pillage by Peter, five months before. But a frontier guard hurried to Nish, where the governor Nicetas was residing and where an escort for Godfrey was waiting. The escort set out at once and met him in the Serbian forest, half-way between Nish and Belgrade. Arrangements for provisioning the army had already been made; and it moved on without trouble through the Balkan peninsula. At Philippopolis news reached it of the arrival of Hugh of Vermandois at Constantinople and of the wonderful gifts that he and his comrades had received. Baldwin of Hainault and Henry of Esch were so deeply impressed that they decided to hasten on ahead of the army to the capital in order to secure their share in the gifts before the others came. But when rumour also reported, not entirely without foundation, that Hugh was being kept a prisoner, Godfrey was somewhat disquieted.

On about 12 December Godfrey's army halted at Selymbria, on the Sea of Marmora. There its discipline, which had hitherto been excellent, suddenly broke down; and for eight days it ravaged the countryside. The reason for this disorder is unknown; but Godfrey sought to excuse it as reprisals for Hugh's imprisonment. The Emperor Alexius promptly sent two Frenchmen in his service, Rudulph Peeldelau and Roger, son of Dagobert, to remonstrate with Godfrey and to persuade him to continue his march in peace. They succeeded; and on 23 December Godfrey's army arrived at Constantinople and encamped, at the request of the Emperor, outside the city along the upper waters of the Golden Horn.

Godfrey's arrival with a large and well-equipped army presented a difficult problem to the imperial government. In pursuit of his policy, Alexius wished to make sure of Godfrey's allegiance and then to send him on as soon as possible out of the dangerous neighbourhood of the capital. It is doubtful whether he really suspected, as his daughter Anna suggests, that Godfrey had designs on Constantinople. But the suburbs of the city had already suffered severely from the ravages of Peter the Hermit's followers. It was dangerous to expose them to the attentions of an army that had proved itself equally lawless and was far better armed. But he had first to secure Godfrey's oath of homage. Accordingly, as soon as Godfrey was settled in his camp, Hugh of Vermandois was sent to visit him, to persuade him to come to see the Emperor. Hugh, so far from resenting his treatment at the Emperor's hands, willingly undertook the mission.

Godfrey refused the Emperor's invitation. He felt out of his depth. Hugh's attitude puzzled him. His troops had already made contact with the remnants of Peter's forces, most of whom justified their recent disaster by attributing it to imperial treachery; and he was affected by their propaganda. As Duke of Lower Lorraine he had taken a personal oath of allegiance to the emperor Henry IV, and may have thought that this precluded an oath to the rival eastern Emperor. Moreover, he did not wish to take any important step till he could consult the other Crusading leaders whom he knew to be soon arriving. Hugh returned to the palace without an answer for Alexius.

Alexius was angry, and unwisely thought to bring Godfrey to reason by shutting off the supplies that he had promised to provide for his troops. While Godfrey hesitated, Baldwin at once began to raid the suburbs, till Alexius promised to lift the blockade. At the same time Godfrey agreed to move his camp down the Golden Horn to Pera, where it would be better sheltered from the winter winds, and where the imperial police could watch it more closely. For some time neither side took further action. The Emperor supplied the western troops with sufficient provisions; and Godfrey for his part saw that discipline was maintained. At the end of January Alexius again invited Godfrey to visit him; but Godfrey was still unwilling to commit himself till other Crusading leaders should join him. He sent his cousin, Baldwin of Le Bourg, Conon of Montaigu and Geoffrey of Esch to the palace to hear the Emperor's proposals, but on their return gave no answer. Alexius was unwilling to provoke Godfrey lest he should again ravage the suburbs. After ensuring that the Lorrainers had no communication with the outside world, he waited till Godfrey should grow impatient and come to terms.

At the end of March Alexius learnt that other Crusading armies would soon arrive at Constantinople. He felt obliged to bring matters to a head, and began to reduce the supplies sent to the Crusaders' camp. First he withheld fodder for their horses, then, as Holy Week approached, their fish and finally bread. The Crusaders responded by making daily raids on the neighbouring villages and eventually came into conflict with the Petcheneg troops that acted as police in the district. In revenge Baldwin set an ambush for the police. Sixty were captured and many of them were put to death. Encouraged by the small success and feeling that he was now committed to fight, Godfrey decided to move his camp and to attack the city itself. After carefully plundering and burning the houses in Pera in which his men had been lodged, he led them across a bridge over the head waters of the Golden Horn, drew them up outside the city walls and began to attack the gate that led to the palace quarter of Blachernae. It is doubtful whether he meant to do more than put pressure on the Emperor; but the Greeks suspected that he aimed at seizing the Empire.

It was the Thursday in Holy Week, 2 April; and Constantinople was quite unprepared for such an onslaught. There were signs of a panic in the city, which was only stilled by the presence and the cool behaviour of the Emperor. He was genuinely shocked by the necessity for fighting on so holy a day. He ordered his troops to make a demonstration outside the gates without coming to blows with the enemy, while his archers on the walls were told to fire over their heads. The Crusaders did not press their attack and soon retired, having slain only seven of the Byzantines. Next day Hugh of Vermandois again went out to remonstrate with Godfrey, who retorted by taunting him with slavishness for having so readily accepted vassaldom. When envoys were sent by Alexius to the camp later in the day to suggest that Godfrey's troops should cross over to Asia even before Godfrey took the oath, the

Crusaders advanced to attack them without waiting to hear what they might say. Thereupon Alexius decided to finish the affair, and flung in more of his men to meet the attack. The Crusaders were no match for the seasoned imperial soldiers. After a brief contest they turned and fled. His defeat brought Godfrey at last to recognize his weakness. He consented both to take the oath of allegiance and to have his army transported across the Bosphorus.

The ceremony of the oath-taking was held probably two days later, on Easter Sunday. Godfrey, Baldwin and their leading lords swore to acknowledge the Emperor as overlord of any conquests that they might make and to hand over to the Emperor's officials any reconquered land that had previously belonged to the Emperor. They then received huge gifts of money and were entertained by the Emperor at a banquet. As soon as the ceremonies were over, Godfrey and his troops were shipped across to Chalcedon and marched on to an encampment at Pelecanum, on the road to Nicomedia.

Alexius had very little time to spare. Already a miscellaneous army, probably composed of various vassals of Godfrey who had preferred to travel through Italy and were probably led by the Count of Toul, had arrived at the outer suburbs of the city and were waiting on the shores of the Marmora, near Sosthenium. They showed the same truculence as Godfrey, and were anxious to wait for Bohemond and the Normans, whom they knew to be close behind; while the Emperor was determined to prevent their junction with Godfrey. It was only after some fighting that he could keep control over their movements; and as soon as Godfrey was safely across the Bosphorus he conveyed them by sea to the capital, where they joined other small groups of Crusaders that had straggled across the Balkans. All the Emperor's tact and many gifts were needed to persuade their leaders to take the oath of allegiance. When at last they consented, Alexius enhanced the solemnity of the occasion by bringing over Godfrey and Baldwin to witness the ceremony. The western lords were grudging and unruly. One of them sat himself down on the Emperor's throne; whereupon Baldwin sharply reproved him, reminding him that he had just become the Emperor's vassal and telling him to observe the customs of the country. The westerner angrily muttered that it was boorish of the Emperor to sit when so many valiant captains were standing. Alexius, who overheard the remark and had it translated for him, asked to speak with the knight; and when the latter began to boast of his unbeaten prowess in single combat, Alexius gently advised him to try other tactics when fighting the Turks.

The incident typified the relations between the Emperor and the Franks. The crude knights from the West were inevitably impressed by the splendour of the palace and by its smooth, careful ceremonial and the quiet, polished manners of the courtiers. But they resented it all. Their wounded pride made them obstreperous and rude, like naughty children.

When their oaths were taken the knights and their men were transported across the straits to join Godfrey's army on the coast of Asia. The Emperor had acted just in time. On 9 April Bohemond of Taranto arrived at Constantinople.

The Normans of southern Italy had not at first taken much notice of Urban's preaching of the Crusade. Intermittent civil war had dragged on there ever since Robert Guiscard's death. Robert had divorced his first wife, Bohemond's mother, and left his duchy of Apulia to his son by Sigelgaita, Roger Borsa. Bohemond revolted against his brother and managed to secure Taranto and the Terra d'Otranto in the heel of the peninsula before their uncle, Roger of Sicily, could patch up an uneasy truce between them. Bohemond never accepted the truce as final and continued surreptitiously to embarrass Roger Borsa. But in the summer of 1096 the whole family had come together to punish the rebel city of Amalfi. The papal decrees about the Crusade had already been published; and small bands of southern Italians had already crossed the sea for the East. But it was only the arrival in Italy of enthusiastic armies of Crusaders from France that made Bohemond realize the importance of the movement. He saw then that it could be used for his advantage. His uncle, Roger of Sicily, would never allow him to annex the whole Apulian duchy. He would do better to find a kingdom in the Levant. The zeal of the French Crusaders affected the Norman troops before Amalfi; and Bohemond encouraged them. He announced that he too would take the Cross and he summoned all good Christians to join him. In front of his assembled army he took off his rich scarlet cloak and tore it into pieces to make crosses for his captains. His vassals hastened to follow his lead, and with them many of his brother's vassals and of the vassals of his uncle of Sicily; who was left complaining that the movement had robbed him of his army.

Bohemond's nephew William started off at once with the French Crusaders; but Bohemond himself needed a little time to prepare his forces. He left his lands under safeguards in his brother's care, and raised sufficient money to pay for the expenses of all that came with him. The expedition sailed from Bari in October. With Bohemond were his nephew Tancred, William's elder brother, son of his sister Emma and the Marquis Odo; his cousins Richard and Rainulf of Salerno and Rainulf's son Richard; Geoffrey, Count of Rossignuolo, and his brothers; Robert of Ansa, Herman of Cannae, Humphrey of Monte Scabioso, Albered of Cagnano and Bishop Girard of Ariano, among the Normans from Sicily; while Normans from France that joined Bohemond included Robert of Sourdeval and Boel of Chartres. His army was smaller than Godfrey's, but it was well equipped and well trained.

The expedition landed in Epirus at various points along the coast between Dyrrhachium and Avlona, and reassembled at a village called Dropoli, up the valley of the river Viusa. The arrangements for landing had doubtless been made after consultation with the Byzantine authorities at Dyrrhachium, who may have wished not to strain any further the resources of the towns along the Via Egnatia; but the choice of the route that his army was to follow was probably Bohemond's. His campaigns fifteen years before had given him some knowledge of the country to the south of the main road; and he may have hoped by taking a less usual route to avoid the supervision of the Byzantines. John Comnenus had no troops to spare; and Bohemond was able to start on his journey without an imperial police escort. But there seems to have been no ill feeling; for

ample supplies were provided for the Normans, while
Bohemond impressed upon all his men that they were to pass
through a Christian land and must refrain from pillage and
disorder.

Travelling right over the passes of the Pindus, the army
reached Castoria, in western Macedonia, shortly before
Christmas. It is impossible to trace his route; but it cannot have
been easy and must have led him over land more than four
thousand feet above sea-level. At Castoria he endeavoured to
secure provisions; but the inhabitants were unwilling to spare
anything from their small stores for those unexpected visitors
whom they remembered as ruthless enemies a few years ago.
The army therefore took the cattle that it required, together
with horses and donkeys, since many of the pack-animals must
have perished on the passes of the Pindus. Christmas was spent
at Castoria; then Bohemond led his men eastward towards the
river Vardar. They paused to attack a village of Paulician
heretics close to their road, burning the houses and their
inmates, and eventually reached the river in the middle of
February, having taken some seven weeks to cover a distance of
little more than a hundred miles.

Bohemond's route probably brought him through Edessa
(Vodena) where he joined the Via Egnatia. Thenceforward he
was accompanied by an escort of Petcheneg soldiers, with the
usual orders from the Emperor to prevent raiding and
straggling and to see that the Crusaders never remained more
than three days at any one place. The Vardar was crossed
without delay by the main portion of the army; but the Count
of Rossignuolo and his brothers delayed with a small party on
the western bank. The Petchenegs therefore attacked them to
urge them on. On hearing of the battle Tancred at once
recrossed the river to rescue them. He drove off the Petchenegs
and made some captives, whom he brought before Bohemond.
Bohemond questioned them; and when he heard that they
were carrying out imperial orders he promptly let them go. His
policy was to behave perfectly correctly towards the Emperor.

In his desire to be correct he had already, probably when he
first landed in Epirus, sent ambassadors ahead to the Emperor.

When his army had passed by the walls of Thessalonica and was on the road to Serres, these ambassadors met him on their return from Constantinople, bringing with them a high imperial official, whose relations with Bohemond soon became cordial. Food was provided in plenty for the army; and in return Bohemond not only promised not to try to enter any of the towns on his route but also agreed to restore all the beasts that his men had taken on their journey. His followers would have liked more than once to raid the countryside; but Bohemond sternly forbade them.

The army reached Roussa (the modern Keshan) in Thrace on 1 April. Bohemond now decided to hurry on to Constantinople, to find out what was being negotiated there between the Emperor and the western leaders that had already arrived. He left his men under the command of Tancred; who took them to a rich valley off the main road, where they spent the Easter weekend. Bohemond came to Constantinople on 9 April. He was lodged outside the walls, at the monastery of St Cosmas and St Damian, and next day was admitted to the presence of the Emperor.

To Alexius Bohemond seemed by far the most dangerous of the Crusaders. Past experience had taught the Byzantines that the Normans were formidable enemies, ambitious, wily and unscrupulous; and Bohemond had shown himself in previous campaigns to be a worthy leader for them. His troops were well organized, well equipped and well disciplined; he had their complete confidence. As a strategist he was perhaps over-sure of himself and not always wise; but as a diplomat he was subtle and persuasive, and far-sighted as a politician. His person was very impressive. Anna Comnena, who knew him and hated him passionately, could not but admit his charm and wrote enthusiastically of his good looks. He was immensely tall; and though he was already over forty years of age, he had the figure and complexion of a young man, broad-shouldered and narrow-waisted, with a clear skin and ruddy cheeks. He wore his yellow hair shorter than was the fashion with western knights and was clean-shaven. He had stooped slightly from his childhood, but without impairing his air of health and strength.

There was, says Anna, something hard in his expression and sinister in his smile; but being, like all Greeks down the ages, susceptible to human beauty, she could not withhold her admiration.

Alexius arranged first to see Bohemond alone, while he discovered what was his attitude; but, finding him perfectly friendly and helpful, he admitted Godfrey and Baldwin, who were still staying in the palace, to take part in the discussions. Bohemond's correctness of behaviour was deliberate. He knew, far better than the other Crusaders, that Byzantium was still very powerful and that without its help nothing could be achieved. To quarrel with it would only lead to disaster; but a wise use of its alliance could be turned to his advantage. He wished to lead the campaign, but he had no authority from the Pope to do so and he would have to contend with the rivalry of the other Crusading chieftains. If he could obtain an official charge from the Emperor he would be in a position from which he could direct operations. He would be in control of the Crusaders' dealings with the Emperor; he would be the functionary to whom the Crusaders would have to hand over the lands reconquered for the Empire. He would be the pivot on which the whole Christian alliance would turn. Without hesitation he took the oath of allegiance to the Emperor and then suggested that he might be appointed to the post of Grand Domestic of the East, that is, commander-in-chief of all the imperial forces in Asia.

The request embarrassed Alexius. He feared and distrusted Bohemond, but was anxious to retain his goodwill. He had already shown him particular generosity and honours, and he continued to pour money on him. But he prevaricated over the request. It was not yet the moment, he said, to make such an appointment, but Bohemond would doubtless earn it by his energy and his loyalty. Bohemond had to be satisfied with this vague promise, which encouraged him to maintain his policy of cooperation. Meanwhile Alexius promised to send troops to accompany the Crusading armies, to repay them for their expenses and to ensure their revictualling and their communications.

Bohemond's army was then summoned to Constantinople and on 26 April it was conveyed across the Bosphorus to join Godfrey's at Pelecanum. Tancred, who disliked and did not understand his uncle's policy, passed through the city by night with his cousin, Richard of Salerno, in order to avoid having to take the oath. That same day Count Raymond of Toulouse arrived at Constantinople and was received by the Emperor.

Raymond IV, Count of Toulouse, usually known from his favourite property as the Count of Saint-Gilles, was already a man of mature age, probably approaching his sixtieth year. His ancestral county was one of the richest in France, and he had recently inherited the equally rich marquisate of Provence. By his marriage with the princess Elvira of Aragon he was connected with the royal houses of Spain; and he had taken part in several holy wars against the Spanish Moslems. He was the only great noble with whom Pope Urban had personally discussed his project of the Crusade, and he was the first to announce his adherence. He therefore considered himself with some justification to be entitled to its lay command. But the Pope, anxious to keep the movement under spiritual control, had never admitted this claim. Raymond probably hoped that the need for a lay leader would become apparent. In the meantime he planned to set out for the East in the company of its spiritual chief, the Bishop of Le Puy.

Raymond had taken the Cross at the time of Clermont, in November 1095; but it was not till next October that he was ready to leave his lands. He vowed to spend the rest of his days in the Holy Land; but it is possible that the vow was made with reservations; for, while he left his lands in France to be administered by his natural son, Bertrand, he carefully did not abdicate his rights. His wife and his legitimate heir, Alfonso, were to accompany him. He sold or pledged some of his lands in order to raise money for his expedition; but he seems to have shown a certain economy in its equipment. His personality is difficult to assess. His actions show him as being vain, obstinate and somewhat rapacious. But his courteous manners impressed the Byzantines, who found him rather more civilized than his colleagues. He also struck them as being more reliable and honest. Anna Comnena, whom later events prejudiced in his favour, commended the superiority of his nature and the purity of his life. Adhemar of Le Puy, who was certainly a man of high standards, clearly regarded him as a worthy friend.

Several noblemen from southern France joined Raymond's Crusade. Amongst these were Rambald, Count of Orange, Gaston of Béarn, Gerard of Roussillon, William of Montpelier, Raymond of Le Forez and Isoard of Gap. Adhemar of Le Puy brought with him his brothers, Francis-Lambert of Monteil, lord of Peyrins, and William-Hugh of Monteil, and all his men. After Adhemar the chief ecclesiastic to come was William, Bishop of Orange.

The expedition crossed the Alps by the Col de Genèvre and travelled through northern Italy to the head of the Adriatic. Perhaps from motives of economy Raymond had decided not to go by sea across the Adriatic but to follow its eastern shore through Istria and Dalmatia. It was an unwise decision; for the Dalmatian roads were very bad and the population rough and unfriendly. Istria was crossed without incident; then for forty winter days the army struggled along the rocky Dalmatian tracks, continually harassed by wild Slav tribes that hung on its rear. Raymond himself remained with the rearguard to protect it, and on one occasion only saved his men by erecting across the road a barrier made of Slav prisoners that he had captured and cruelly mutilated. He had started out well supplied with foodstuffs; and none of his men perished on the journey from hunger nor in the fighting. When at last they reached Skodra, supplies were running low. Raymond obtained an interview with the local Serbian prince, Bodin, who in return for costly presents agreed to allow the Crusaders to buy freely in the markets of the town. But no food was available. The army had to continue on its way in growing hunger and misery till it reached the imperial frontier north of Dyrrhachium early in February. Raymond and Adhemar now hoped that their troubles were at an end.

John Comnenus welcomed the Crusaders at Dyrrhachium, where imperial envoys and a Petcheneg escort were waiting to convey them along the Via Egnatia. Raymond sent an embassy ahead to Constantinople to announce his arrival; and after a few days' rest at Dyrrhachium the army set out again. Adhemar's brother, the lord of Peyrins, was left behind to recover from an illness caused by the hardships of the journey. Raymond's men were unruly and ill-disciplined. They resented the presence of Petcheneg police watching them on every side; and their incorrigible taste for marauding brought them into frequent conflict with their escort. Before many days had passed two Provençal barons were killed in one of these skirmishes. Soon afterwards the Bishop of Le Puy himself strayed from the road and was wounded and captured by the Petchenegs before they realized who he was. He was promptly returned to the army, and seems to have borne no resentment for the incident; but the troops were deeply shocked. Their ill temper increased when Raymond himself was attacked in similar circumstances near Edessa.

At Thessalonica the Bishop of Le Puy left the army in order to receive proper treatment for his wounds. He remained there till his brother was able to join him from Dyrrhachium. Without his restraining influence the discipline of the army worsened; but there was no serious mishap till it reached Roussa in Thrace. Bohemond's men had been delighted with their reception at this town a fortnight earlier; but, perhaps because the townsfolk had no provisions left for sale, Raymond's men took offence at something. Crying 'Toulouse, Toulouse' they attacked the walls and forced an entrance and pillaged all the houses. At Rodosto a few days later they were met by Raymond's ambassadors returning from Constantinople with an envoy from the Emperor and cordial messages urging Raymond to hasten to the capital and adding that Bohemond and Godfrey were eager for his presence. It was probably the latter part of the message and the fear of being absent while important decisions were made that induced Raymond to accept the invitation. He left his army and hurried ahead to Constantinople where he arrived on 21 April.

With his departure there was no one to keep the army in order. It began at once to raid the countryside. But now there was more than a small Petcheneg escort to oppose it. Regiments of the Byzantine army, stationed nearby, moved up to attack the raiders. In the battle that followed Raymond's men were thoroughly defeated and fled, leaving their arms and their baggage in the hands of the Byzantines. The news of the disaster reached Raymond just as he was setting out to interview the Emperor.

Raymond had been well received at Constantinople. He was housed in a palace just outside the walls but was begged to come as soon as possible to the palace, where it was suggested that he should take the oath of allegiance. But the experiences of his journey and the news that he had just received had put him in an ill temper; and he was puzzled and displeased by the situation that he found in the palace. His everlasting aim was to be recognized as military leader of the whole Crusading expedition. But his authority, such as it was, came from the Pope and from his connection with the papal representative, the Bishop of Le Puy. The bishop was absent. Raymond lacked both the support and the advice that his presence would have given. Without him he was unwilling to commit himself; the more so, as to take the oath of allegiance as the other Crusaders had done would mean the abandonment of his special relation towards the Papacy. He would reduce himself to the same level as the others. There was a further danger. He was intelligent enough to see at once that Bohemond was his most dangerous rival. Bohemond seemed to be enjoying the particular favours of the Emperor; and it was rumoured that he was to be appointed to a high imperial command. To take the oath might mean that not only would Raymond lose his priority but he might well find himself under the jurisdiction of Bohemond as the Emperor's representative. He declared that he had come to the East to do God's work and that God was now his only suzerain, implying thereby that he was the lay delegate of the Pope. But he added that if the Emperor were himself to lead the united Christian forces, he would serve under him. The concession shows that it was not the Emperor but Bohemond that he resented. The Emperor could only reply that unfortunately the state of the Empire would not permit him to leave it. In vain the other western leaders, fearing that the success of the whole campaign was in jeopardy, begged Raymond to change his mind. Bohemond, hoping still for the imperial command and eager to please the Emperor, went so far as to say that he would support the Emperor should Raymond openly quarrel with him; while even Godfrey pointed out the harm that his attitude was doing to the Christian cause. Alexius himself kept apart from the discussions, though he withheld from Raymond such gifts as he had given to the other princes. At last, on 26 April, Raymond agreed to swear a modified oath, promising to respect the life and honour of the Emperor and to see that nothing was done, by himself or by his men, that would be to his hurt. This type of oath was not unusual for vassals to take in southern France; and with it Alexius was satisfied.

It was when these negotiations were over that Bohemond and his army crossed into Asia. Meanwhile, Raymond's army had reassembled, rather crestfallen, at Rodosto, where it awaited the arrival of the Bishop of Le Puy who was to lead it on to Constantinople. Of Adhemar's activities in the capital we know nothing. Presumably he saw the chief Greek ecclesiastics; and he certainly had an audience with the Emperor. These interviews were very friendly. He may have helped to reconcile Raymond with Alexius; for their relations quickly improved. But it is probable that Bohemond's departure was of great assistance. The Emperor was able to see Raymond in private and to explain to him that he too had no love for the Normans and that Bohemond would in fact never receive an imperial command. Raymond took his army across the Bosphorus two days after taking his oath, but returned to spend a fortnight at the court. When he left he was on cordial terms with Alexius, in whom he knew now that he had a powerful ally against Bohemond. His attitude towards the Empire was altered.

The fourth great western army to go on the Crusade set out from northern France in October 1096, shortly after Raymond had left his home. It was under the joint leadership of Robert, Duke of Normandy, his brother-in-law Stephen, Count of Blois, and his cousin Robert II, Count of Flanders. Robert of Normandy was the eldest son of William the Conqueror. He was a man of forty, mild-mannered and somewhat ineffectual, but not without personal courage and charm. Ever since his father's death he had been carrying on a desultory war with his brother, William Rufus of England, who had several times invaded his duchy. Urban's preaching of the Crusade had deeply moved him; and he soon declared his adhesion. In return the Pope, while he was still in northern France, arranged a reconciliation between him and his brother. But Robert took several months to plan his Crusade and was eventually only able to raise the money that he required by pledging his duchy to William for ten thousand silver marks. The act confirming the pledge was signed in September 1096. A few days later Robert set out with his army for Pontarlier, where he was joined by Stephen of Blois and Robert of Flanders. With him were Odo, Bishop of Bayeux, Walter, Count of Saint-Valéry, the heirs of the Counts of Montgomery and Mortagne, Girard of Gournay, Hugh of Saint-Pol and the sons of Hugh of Grant-Mesnil, and a number of knights and infantrymen not only from Normandy but also from England, Scotland and Brittany; though the only English nobleman to accompany the Crusade, Ralph Guader, Earl of Norfolk, was at the time an exile, living on his mother's estates in Brittany.

Stephen of Blois had no desire to join the Crusade. But he had married Adela, daughter of William the Conqueror; and in their household it was she who made the decisions. She wished him to go; and he went. With him were his chief vassals, Everard of Le Puits, Guerin Gueronat, Caro Asini, Geoffrey Guerin, and his chaplain Alexander. Amongst the party was the cleric Fulcher of Chartres, the future historian. Stephen, who was one of the wealthiest men in France, raised the money for his journey without great difficulty. He left his lands in the competent management of his wife.

The Count of Flanders was a slightly younger man but possessed a more formidable personality. His father, Robert I, had made the pilgrimage to Jerusalem in 1086, and on his way back had taken service for a while under the Emperor Alexius, with whom he remained in touch until his death in 1093. It was therefore natural that Robert II should wish to carry on his work against the infidel. His army was a little smaller than

Raymond's or Godfrey's but was of high quality. He was accompanied by troops from Brabant, under Baldwin of Alost, Count of Ghent. His lands were to be administered in his absence by his countess, Clementia of Burgundy.

From Pontarlier the united army moved southward across the Alps into Italy. Passing through Lucca in November it met Pope Urban, who was staying there a few days on his way from Cremona to Rome. Urban received the leaders in audience and gave them his special blessing. The army went on to Rome, to visit the tomb of Saint Peter, but refused to interfere in the struggle between Urban's followers and the followers of the anti-Pope Guibert which was troubling the city. From Rome it passed, by way of Monte Cassino, into the Norman duchy in the south. There it was well received by the Duke of Apulia, Roger Borsa, whose wife, Adela, the widowed queen of Denmark, was the Count of Flanders' sister, and who acknowledged the Duke of Normandy as the head of his race. Roger offered his brother-in-law many costly gifts; but the latter would only accept a present of holy relics, the hair of the Virgin and the bones of Saint Matthew and Saint Nicholas, which he sent to his wife to place in the abbey of Watten.

Robert of Normandy and Stephen of Blois decided to spend the winter comfortably in Calabria. But Robert of Flanders moved on almost at once to Bari with his men and crossed over into Epirus, early in December. He reached Constantinople without any untoward incident about the same time as Bohemond. But the Count of Alost, who had attempted to land near Chimarra, further south than the accepted ports of disembarkation, found his way blocked by a Byzantine squadron. There was a slight sea-battle, recounted at length in Anna Comnena's history, as its hero, Marianus Mavrocatacalon, the son of the admiral, was a friend of hers. In spite of the prowess of a Latin priest, whose warlike disregard of his cloth shocked the Byzantines, the Brabançon ship was boarded and captured; and the Count and his men were landed at Dyrrhachium. The Flemish party apparently made no difficulty about the oath of allegiance to Alexius. Count Robert was among the princes that urged Raymond to comply.

Robert of Normandy and Stephen of Blois lingered on in

southern Italy till the spring. Their lack of enthusiasm affected their followers, many of whom began to wander back towards their homes. At last, in March, the army moved to Brindisi, and on 5 April it prepared to embark. Unfortunately, the first ship to set sail capsized and foundered, losing some four hundred passengers, with their horses and mules and many chests of money. The tactful discovery that the corpses washed up on the shore were miraculously marked with crosses on their shoulder-blades, while it edified the faithful, did not discourage many more timorous folk from abandoning the expedition. But the bulk of the army safely embarked and after a rough voyage of four days landed at Dyrrhachium. The Byzantine authorities received them well and provided them with an escort to take them along the Via Egnatia to Constantinople. Apart from an accident while the army was crossing a stream in the Pindus, when a sudden flood swept away several pilgrims, the journey passed pleasantly. After a delay of four days before the walls of Thessalonica, Constantinople was reached early in May. A camp was provided for the army just outside the walls; and parties of five or six at a time were admitted daily into the city to see its sights and worship at its shrines. The earlier Crusading armies had all by now been transferred across the Bosphorus; and these latecomers found no malcontents to spoil their relations with the Byzantines. They were struck with admiration at the beauty and splendour of the city; they enjoyed the rest and comfort that it provided. They were grateful for the Emperor's distribution of coins and of silk garments and for the food and the horses that he provided. Their leaders at once took the oath of allegiance to the Emperor and were rewarded with magnificent presents. Stephen of Blois, writing next month to his wife, to whom he was a dutiful correspondent, was in ecstasies over his reception by the Emperor. He stayed for ten days at the palace, where the Emperor treated him like a son, giving him much good advice and many superb gifts and offering to educate his youngest son. Stephen was particularly impressed by the Emperor's generosity to all ranks in the Crusading army and by his lavish and efficient organization of supplies for the troops already in the field. 'Your father, my love', he wrote, alluding to William the Conqueror, 'made many great gifts, but he was almost nothing compared to this man.'

The army spent a fortnight at Constantinople before it was transported to Asia. Even the crossing of the Bosphorus pleased Stephen, who had heard that the channel was dangerous but found it no more so than the Marne or the Seine. They marched along the Gulf of Nicomedia, past Nicomedia itself, to join the main Crusading armies, who were already beginning the siege of Nicaea.

Alexius could breathe again. He had wished for mercenaries from the West. Instead, he had been sent large armies, each with its own leaders. No government really cares to find numbers of independent allied forces invading its territory, particularly when they are on a lower level of civilization. Food had to be provided; marauding had to be prevented. The actual size of the Crusading armies can only be conjectured. Medieval estimates are always exaggerated; but Peter the Hermit's rabble, including its many non-combatants, probably approached twenty thousand. The chief Crusading armies, Raymond's, Godfrey's and the northern French, each numbered well over ten thousand, including non-combatants. Bohemond's was a little smaller; and there were other lesser groups. But in all from sixty to a hundred thousand persons must have entered the Empire from the West between the summer of 1096 and the spring of 1097. On the whole the Emperor's arrangements for dealing with them had succeeded. None of the Crusaders had suffered from lack of food when crossing the Balkans. The only raids made to secure food were those of Walter Sans-Avoir at Belgrade and Peter at Bela Palanka, both under exceptional circumstances, and of Bohemond at Castoria, when he was travelling in midwinter along an unsuitable road. Petty marauding and one or two wanton attacks on towns had been impossible to prevent, as Alexius had insufficient troops for the purpose. But his Petcheneg squadrons, by their blind uncompromising obedience to orders, irritating though it must have been to the Crusaders, proved an efficient police force; while his special envoys usually handled the western princes with tact. The growing success of the Emperor's methods is shown by the smooth passage of the last of the armies, composed of northern Frenchmen, who were not a well-disciplined people and were led by weak and incompetent leaders.

At Constantinople Alexius had obtained an oath of allegiance from all the princes except Raymond, with whom he had achieved a private understanding. He had no illusions about the practical value of the oath nor about the reliability of the men that had sworn it. But at least it gave him a juridical advantage that might well prove important. The result had not been easy to achieve; for though the wiser leaders, such as Bohemond, and intelligent observers, such as Fulcher of Chartres, saw the necessity for cooperation with Byzantium, to the lesser knights and the rank and file the oath seemed to be an humiliation and even a betrayal of trust. They had been prejudiced against the Byzantines by the chilly welcome that they had received from the countryfolk, whom they thought that they were coming to save. Constantinople, that vast, splendid city, with all its wealth, its busy population of merchants and manufacturers, its courtly nobles in their civilian robes and the richly dressed, painted great ladies with their trains of eunuchs and slaves, roused in them contempt mixed with an uncomfortable sense of inferiority. They could not understand the language nor the customs of the country. Even the church services were alien to them.

Byzantines returned their dislike. To the citizens of the capital these rough, unruly brigands, encamped for so long in their suburbs, were an unmitigated nuisance; while the attitude of the countryfolk is shown in a letter written by Theophylact, Archbishop of Bulgaria, from his see of Ochrida, on the Via Egnatia. Theophylact, who was notoriously broadminded towards the West, speaks of the trouble caused by the passage of the Crusaders through his diocese, but adds that now he and his folk were learning to bear the burden with patience. The opening of the Crusade did not augur well for the good relations between East and West.

Nevertheless, Alexius was probably not ill satisfied. The

danger to Constantinople was over; and the great Crusading army had set out to fight against the Turks. He intended genuinely to cooperate with the Crusade, but with one qualification. He would not sacrifice the interests of the Empire to the interests of the western knights. His duty was first to his own people. Moreover, like all Byzantines, he believed that the welfare of Christendom depended on the welfare of the historic Christian Empire. His belief was correct.

CHAPTER 9

The campaign in Asia Minor

And thou shalt come from thy place out of the north parts, thou, and many people with thee, all of them riding on horses, a great company, and mighty army.

Ezekiel xxxviii, 15

However much the Emperor and the Crusader princes might quarrel over their ultimate rights and the distribution of conquests to come, there could be no dissension about the opening stages of the campaign against the infidel. If the Crusade was to reach Jerusalem, the roads across Asia Minor must be cleared; and to drive the Turk out of Asia Minor was the chief aim of Byzantine policy. There was complete agreement on strategy; and as yet, with a Byzantine army by their side, the Crusaders were willing to defer to its experienced generals on matters of tactics.

The first objective was the Seldjuk capital, Nicaea. Nicaea lay on the shores of the Ascanian lake, not far from the Sea of Marmora. The old Byzantine Military road ran through it, though there was an alternative route passing a little further to the east. To leave this great fortress in enemy hands would endanger all communications across the country. Alexius was eager to move the Crusaders on as soon as possible, as summer was advancing; and the Crusaders themselves were impatient. In the last days of April, before the northern French army had arrived at Constantinople, orders were given to prepare to strike the camp at Pelecanum and to advance on Nicaea.

The moment was well chosen; for the Seldjuk Sultan, Kilij Arslan I, was away on his eastern frontier, contesting with the Danishmend princes for the suzerainty of Melitene, whose

Armenian ruler, Gabriel, was busily embroiling the neighbouring potentates with each other. Kilij Arslan did not take
seriously this new menace from the West. His easy defeat of
Peter the Hermit's rabble taught him to despise the Crusaders;
and perhaps his spies in Constantinople, wishing to please their
master, gave him exaggerated accounts of the quarrels between
the Emperor and the western princes. Believing that the
Crusade would never penetrate to Nicaea, he left his wife and
children and all his treasure inside its walls. It was only when
he received news of the enemy concentration at Pelecanum that
he sent part of his army hurrying back westward, following
himself as soon as he could arrange his affairs in the east. His
troops arrived too late to interfere with the Crusaders' march
on Nicaea.

Godfrey of Lorraine's army left Pelecanum on about 26
April, and marched to Nicomedia, where it waited for three
days and was joined by Bohemond's army, under the command
of Tancred, and by Peter the Hermit and the remains of his
rabble. Bohemond himself stayed on for a few days at
Constantinople, to arrange with the Emperor for the provision
of supplies to the army. A small Byzantine detachment of
engineers with siege engines accompanied the troops, under the
leadership of Manuel Butumites. From Nicomedia Godfrey led
the army to Civetot, then turned south through the defile
where Peter's men had perished. Their bones still covered the
entrance to the pass; and, warned by their fate and by the
advice of the Emperor, Godfrey moved cautiously, sending
scouts and engineers in front, to clear and widen the track;
which was then marked by a series of wooden crosses, to serve
as a guide for future pilgrims. On 6 May he arrived before
Nicaea. The city had been strongly fortified since the fourth
century; and its walls, some four miles in length, with their two
hundred and forty towers, had been kept in constant repair by
the Byzantines. It lay on the eastern end of the Ascanian Lake,
its west walls rising straight out of the shallow water, and it
formed an uneven pentagon. Godfrey encamped outside the
northern wall and Tancred outside the eastern wall. The
southern wall was left for Raymond's army.

The Turkish garrison was large but needed reinforcements.

Messengers, one of whom was intercepted by the Crusaders, were sent to the Sultan to urge him to rush troops into the city through the south gates, before its investment was complete. But the Turkish army was still too far away. Before its vanguard could approach, Raymond arrived, on 16 May, and spread his army before the southern wall. Bohemond had joined his army two or three days sooner. Till he came, insufficient provisions had weakened the Crusaders; but, thanks to his arrangements with Alexius, henceforward supplies flowed freely to the besiegers, coming both by land and by sea. When Robert of Normandy and Stephen of Blois arrived with their forces on 3 June, the whole Crusading army was assembled. It worked together as a single unit, though there was no one supreme commander. Decisions were taken by the princes acting in council. As yet there was no serious discord between them. Meanwhile the Emperor moved out to Pelecanum, where he could keep in touch both with his capital and with Nicaea.

The first Turkish relieving force reached Nicaea immediately after Raymond, to find the city entirely blockaded by land. After a brief, unsuccessful skirmish with Raymond's troops it withdrew, to await the main Turkish army which was approaching under the leadership of the Sultan. Alexius had instructed Butumites to establish contact with the besieged garrison. When it saw its relief retreating, its leaders invited Butumites under a safe conduct into the town, to discuss terms of surrender. He accepted; but almost at once news came that the Sultan was not far away; and negotiations were broken off.

It was on about 21 May that the Sultan and his army came up from the south and at once attacked the Crusaders in an attempt to force an entrance into the city. Raymond, with the Bishop of Le Puy in command of his right flank, bore the brunt of the attack; for neither Godfrey nor Bohemond could venture to leave his section of the walls unguarded. But Robert of Flanders and his troops came to Raymond's aid. The battle raged fiercely all day; but the Turks could make no headway. When night fell the Sultan decided to retreat. The Crusader army was stronger than he had thought; and, man for man, his Turks were no match for the well-armed westerners in the open

ground in front of the city. It was better strategy to retreat into
the mountains and to leave the city to its fate.

The Crusaders' losses had been heavy. Many had been
killed, including Baldwin, Count of Ghent; and almost all the
surviving participants in the battle had been wounded. But the
victory filled them with elation. To their delight they found
among the Turkish dead the ropes brought to bind the
prisoners that the Sultan had hoped to take. To weaken the
morale of the besieged garrison they cut off the heads of many
of the enemy corpses and threw them over the walls or fixed
them on pikes to parade them before the gates. Then, with no
more danger to fear from outside, they concentrated on the
siege. But the fortifications were formidable. In vain Raymond
and Adhemar attempted to mine one of the southern towers by
sending sappers to dig beneath it and there to light a huge fire.
The little damage that was done was repaired during the night
by the garrison. Moreover it was found that the blockade was
incomplete; for supplies still reached the city from across the
lake. The Crusaders were obliged to ask the Emperor to come
to their help and to provide boats to intercept this water route.
Alexius was probably well aware of the position but wished the
western princes to discover how necessary his cooperation was
to them. At their request he provided a small flotilla for the
lake, under the command of Butumites.

The Sultan, when he retired, had told the garrison to do as
it thought best, as he could give no more aid. When it saw the
Byzantine ships on the lake and understood that the Emperor
was fully assisting the Crusaders it decided upon surrender.
This was what Alexius had hoped. He had no wish to add a
half-destroyed city to his dominions nor that his future subjects
should undergo the horrors of a sack, especially as the majority
of the citizens were Christians; for the Turks comprised only
the soldiers and a small Court nobility. Contact was re-
established with Butumites, and the terms of surrender were
discussed. But the Turks still hesitated, hoping, perhaps, that
the Sultan would return. It was only on the news that the
Crusaders were planning a general assault that at last they gave
in.

The assault was ordered for 19 June. But when morning

broke the Crusaders saw the Emperor's standard waving over the city towers. The Turks had surrendered during the night; and imperial troops, mainly Petcheneg, had entered the city through the gates on the lakeside. It is unlikely that the Crusading leaders had not been informed of the negotiations; nor did they disapprove, for they saw that it was pointless to waste time and men on storming a town that would not be theirs to hold. But they were deliberately kept in ignorance of the final stages; while the rank and file considered themselves cheated of their prey. They had hoped to pillage the riches of Nicaea. Instead, they were only allowed in small groups into the city, closely surveyed by the Emperor's police. They had hoped to hold the Turkish nobles up to ransom. Instead, they saw them conveyed under escort, with their movable possessions, to Constantinople or to the Emperor at Pelecanum. Their resentment against the Emperor grew more bitter.

To some extent it was mitigated by the Emperor's generosity. For Alexius promptly ordered that a gift of food should be made to every Crusading soldier, while the leaders were summoned to Pelecanum, to be presented with gold and with jewels from the Sultan's treasury. Stephen of Blois, who travelled there with Raymond of Toulouse, was awestricken by the mountain of gold that was his portion. He did not share the view, held by some of his comrades, that the Emperor should have come in person to Nicaea, for he understood that the demonstration that the liberated city would make to receive its sovereign might prove embarrassing to him. In return for his presents Alexius required the knights who had not yet taken the oath of allegiance to him to do so now. Many lesser lords, about whom he had not troubled when they passed through Constantinople, complied. Raymond was not, it seems, asked to do more than he had already done; but Tancred's case was taken more seriously. Tancred at first was truculent. He declared that unless the Emperor's great tent was given to him filled to the brim with gold, as well as an amount equal to all the gold given to the other princes, he would swear nothing. When the Emperor's brother-in-law, George Palaeologus, protested at his rudeness, he turned roughly on him and began to manhandle him. The Emperor rose to intervene, and Bohemond sharply reproved his nephew. In the end Tancred grudgingly paid homage.

The Crusaders were shocked by the Emperor's treatment of his Turkish captives. The court officials and the commanders were allowed to buy their freedom; while the Sultana, the daughter of the Emir Chaka, was received with royal honours at Constantinople, where she was to remain till a message should come from her husband stating where he wished her to join him. She and her children were then to be dispatched to him without ransom. Alexius was a kindly man, and he well knew the value of courtesy to a defeated enemy; but to the western princes his attitude seemed doublefaced and disloyal.

Nevertheless, in spite of some disappointment that they had not themselves captured the city nor helped themselves to its riches, the liberation of Nicaea filled the Crusaders with joy and with hope for the future. Letters went westward to announce that this venerable place was Christian once more; and the news was received with enthusiasm. The Crusade was proved to be a success. More recruits came forward; and the Italian cities, hitherto rather cautious and dilatory with their promised aid, began to take the movement more seriously. In the Crusader camp the knights were eager to continue their journey. Stephen of Blois was full of optimism. 'In five weeks' time', he wrote to his wife, 'we shall be at Jerusalem; unless', he added, more prophetically than he knew, 'we are held up at Antioch.'

From Nicaea the Crusaders set out along the old Byzantine main road across Asia Minor. The road from Chalcedon and Nicomedia joined the road from Helenopolis and Nicaea on the banks of the river Sangarius. It soon left the river to climb up a tributary valley to the south, past the modern Biledjik, then wound over a pass to Dorylaeum, near the modern Eskishehir. There it split into three. The great military road of the Byzantines ran due east, probably by-passing Ancyra to the south, and dividing again, after it crossed the Halys, one branch continuing straight past Sebastea (Sivas) into Armenia, the other turning towards Caesarea Mazacha. From there several roads led across the passes of the Anti-Taurus range into the Euphrates valley, while another road doubled back to the southwest, through Tyana to the Cilician Gates. The second road from Dorylaeum led directly across the great salt desert in the centre of Asia Minor, just south of Lake Tatta, from Amorium to the Cilician Gates. It was a road that could only be used by swiftly moving companies; for it passed through a desolate country entirely lacking in water. The third road skirted the southern edge of the salt desert, running from Philomelium, the modern Akshehir, to Iconium and Heraclea and the Cilician Gates. One branch road led from near Philomelium to the Mediterranean at Attalia, another from just beyond Iconium to the Mediterranean at Seleucia.

Whichever road the Crusading forces should decide to take, they must first reach Dorylaeum. On 26 June, a week after the fall of Nicaea, the vanguard began to move, followed during the next two days by the various divisions of the army, to reassemble at the bridge across the Blue River; where the road leaves the Sangarius valley to climb up into the plateau. A small Byzantine detachment under the experienced general Taticius accompanied the Crusaders. A certain number of the Crusaders, probably for the most part those that had been wounded at Nicaea, stayed behind and took service with the Emperor. They were put under Butumites and employed to repair and to garrison Nicaea.

By the bridge, at a village called Leuce, the princes took counsel. It was decided to divide the army into two sections, in order to ease the problem of supplies, one section to precede the other at about a day's interval. The first army consisted of the Normans of southern Italy and of northern France, with the troops of the Counts of Flanders and of Blois and the Byzantines, who were providing the guides. The second army included the southern French and the Lorrainers, with the troops of the Count of Vermandois. Bohemond was regarded as leader of the first group and Raymond of Toulouse of the second. As soon as the division was made, Bohemond's army set out along the road to Dorylaeum.

After his failure to relieve Nicaea the Sultan Kilij Arslan had withdrawn eastward, to gather his own forces and to conclude peace and an alliance with the Danishmend Emir against this new menace. The loss of Nicaea had alarmed him; and the loss of his treasury there had been serious. But the Turks were still nomadic by instinct. The Sultan's real capital was his tent. In the last days of June he returned towards the west, with all his own troops, with his vassal Hasan, Emir of the Cappadocian Turks, and with the Danishmend army, under its Emir. On 30 June he was waiting in a valley by Dorylaeum, ready to attack the Crusaders as they came down the pass.

That evening the first Crusading army encamped in the plain not far from Dorylaeum. At sunrise the Turks swooped down over the hillside, shouting their battlecry. Bohemond was not unprepared. The non-combatant pilgrims were quickly assembled in the centre of the camp, where there were springs of water; and the women were given the task of carrying water up to the front line. Tents were quickly dressed, and the knights were told to dismount from their horses. Meanwhile a messenger was sent galloping down to the second army, urging it to make haste, while Bohemond addressed his captains, telling them to prepare for a difficult fight and to remain at first on the defensive. Only one of them disobeyed his orders, the same knight that had boldly seated himself on the Emperor's throne at Constantinople. With forty of his men he charged the enemy, to be driven back in ignominy covered with wounds. The camp was soon surrounded by the Turks, whose numbers seemed to the Christians to be infinite, and who followed their favourite tactics of running archers to the front line to discharge their arrows and then at once to make room for others.

As the hot July morning advanced the Crusaders began to doubt whether they could hold out against the ceaseless rain of missiles. But, surrounded as they were, flight was impossible and surrender would mean captivity and slavery. They all determined if need be to suffer martyrdom together. At last, about midday, they saw their comrades of the second army arrive, Godfrey and Hugh and their men in front and Raymond and his men close behind. The Turks had not realized that they had not entrapped the whole Crusading force. At the sight of

the newcomers they faltered and could not prevent the two
armies from making a juncture. The Crusaders were heartened.
Forming a long front with Bohemond, Robert of Normandy
and Stephen of Blois on the left, with Raymond and Robert of
Flanders in the centre, and with Godfrey and Hugh on their
right, they began to take the offensive, reminding each other of
the riches that they would acquire if they were victorious. The
Turks were unprepared to meet an attack and were probably
running short of ammunition. Their hesitation was turned to
panic by the sudden appearance of the Bishop of Le Puy and
a contingent of the southern French on the hills behind them.
Adhemar had himself planned this diversion and found guides
to take him over the mountain paths. His intervention ensured
the Crusaders' triumph. The Turks broke their lines and soon
were in full flight to the east. In their haste they abandoned
their encampment intact; and the tents of the Sultan and the
Emirs fell, with all their treasure, into the hands of the
Christians.

It was a great victory. Many Christian lives had been lost,
including those of Tancred's brother William, of Humphrey of
Monte Scabioso and of Robert of Paris; and the Franks had
been taught to pay a proper respect to the Turks as soldiers.
Perhaps to enhance their achievement, they willingly gave to
the Turks an admiration which they withheld from the
Byzantines, whose more scientific methods of warfare they
regarded as decadent. Nor did they acknowledge the share
taken by the Byzantines in the battle. The anonymous Norman
author of the *Gesta* considered that the Turks would be the finest
of races if only they were Christians; and he recalled the legend
that made the Franks and Turks akin, being both the
descendants of the Trojans – a legend based rather on a
common rivalry against the Greeks than on any ethnological
foundation. But, admirable though the Turkish soldiery might
be, their defeat ensured the safe passage of the Crusaders across
Asia Minor. The Sultan, robbed first of his capital city and now
of his royal tent and the greater part of his treasure, decided
that it was useless to attempt to hold them up. Meeting in his
flight a company of Syrian Turks who had come up too late for

the battle, he explained that the numbers and strength of the Franks were greater than he had expected and that he could not oppose them. He and his people took to the hills after pillaging and deserting the cities that they had occupied and ravaging the countryside, that the Crusaders might find it impossible to feed themselves as they advanced.

The Crusading army rested for two days at Dorylaeum, to recover from the battle and to plan the next stages of the march. The choice of the road to be taken was not difficult. The military road to the east ran too far into country controlled by the Danishmends and by Emirs whose power had not been broken. The army was too large and too slow-moving to cut straight across the salt desert. It had to follow the slower road along the edge of the mountains to the south of the desert. This was no doubt the advice given by Taticius and the guides that he provided. But, even so, the road was uncertain. With the Turcoman invasions and twenty years of warfare, villages had been destroyed and fields gone out of cultivation; wells had become impure or been allowed to dry; bridges had fallen or been destroyed. Information could not always be extracted from the sparse and terrified population. Yet if anything went wrong the Franks at once suspected the Greek guides of treachery, while the Greeks were embittered by Frankish indiscipline and ingratitude. Taticius found his role increasingly unpleasant and difficult.

Starting out on 3 July in one continuous body, to avoid a recurrence of the risk run at Dorylaeum, the army toiled southeastward across the Anatolian plateau. It could not keep to the old main road. After passing through Polybotus it turned off to Pisidian Antioch, which had probably escaped devastation by the Turks, and where supplies could therefore be obtained. Thence the Crusaders crossed over the bare passes of the Sultan Dagh to rejoin the main road at Philomelium. From Philomelium their way ran through desolate country between the mountains and the desert. In the relentless heat of high summer the heavily armed knights and their horses and the foot-soldiers all suffered terribly. There was no water to be seen except the salt marshes of the desert and no vegetation except thorn bushes, whose branches they chewed in a vain attempt to find moisture. They could see the old Byzantine cisterns by the roadside; but they had all been ruined by the Turks. The horses were the first to perish. Many knights were forced to go on foot; others could be seen riding on oxen; while sheep and goats and dogs were collected to pull the baggage trains. But the morale of the army remained high. To Fulcher of Chartres the comradeship of the soldiers, coming from so many different lands and speaking so many different languages, seemed something inspired by God.

In the middle of August the Crusaders reached Iconium. Iconium, the Konya of today, had been in Turkish hands for thirteen years; and Kilij Arslan was soon to choose it as his new capital. But at the moment it was deserted. The Turks had fled into the mountains with all their movable possessions. But they could not destroy the streams and orchards in the delicious valley of Meram, behind the city. Its fertility enchanted the weary Christians. They rested there for several days to recover their strength. All of them were in need of rest. Even their leaders were worn out. Godfrey had been wounded a few days earlier by a bear that he was hunting. Raymond of Toulouse was gravely ill, and was thought to be dying. The Bishop of Orange gave him extreme unction; but the sojourn at Iconium restored him, and he was able to march with the army when it moved on. Taking the advice of the small population of Armenians living near Iconium, the soldiers took with them sufficient water to last them till they reached the fertile valley of Heraclea.

At Heraclea they found a Turkish army, under the Emir Hasan and the Danishmend Emir. The two Emirs, anxious for their possessions in Cappadocia, probably hoped by their presence to force the Crusaders to attempt to cross the Taurus mountains to the coast. But at the sight of the Turks the Crusaders at once attacked, led by Bohemond, who sought out the Danishmend Emir himself. The Turks had no desire for a pitched battle and swiftly retired to the north, abandoning the towns to the Christians. A comet flaring through the sky illuminated the victory.

It was now necessary to discuss again the route to be followed. A little to the east of Heraclea the main road led across the Taurus mountains, through the tremendous pass of the Cilician Gates, into Cilicia. This was the direct route to Antioch; but it offered disadvantages. The Cilician Gates are not easy to cross. At times the road is so steep and so narrow that a small hostile party in command of the heights can quickly cause havoc to a slowmoving army. Cilicia was in Turkish hands; and the climate there in September, as the Byzantine guides could report, is at its deadliest. Moreover, an army going from Cilicia to Antioch must cross over the Amanus range, by the difficult pass known as the Syrian Gates. On the other hand, the recent defeat of the Turks opened the road to Caesarea Mazacha. From there a continuation of the great Byzantine military road led across Anti-Taurus to Marash (Germanicea) and down over the low broad pass of the Amanus Gates into the plain of Antioch. This was the road that traffic from Antioch to Constantinople had mainly taken in the years before the Turkish invasions; and at the moment it had the advantage of passing through country held by Christians, Armenian princelings, for the most part nominal vassals of the Emperor and likely to be well disposed. It is probable that this latter route was recommended by Taticius and the Byzantines, but their suggestion was opposed by those of the princes that were hostile to the Emperor, led by Tancred. The majority decided to take the road through Caesarea. But Tancred, with a body of the Normans of southern Italy, and Godfrey's brother Baldwin, with some of the Flemish and of the Lorrainers, determined to split from the main army and to cross into Cilicia.

About 10 September Tancred and Baldwin set off by two separate routes for the Taurus passes, and the main army moved northeastward towards Caesarea. At the village of Augustopolis it caught up with Hasan's troops and inflicted another defeat on them; but, wishing to avoid delay, it did not attempt to capture a castle of the Emir's that stood not far from the road; though several small villages were occupied and were given to a local Armenian lord, by name Symeon, at his own

request, to hold under the Emperor. At the end of the month
the Crusaders reached Caesarea, which had been deserted by
the Turks. They did not stop there but moved on to Comana
(Placentia), a prosperous town inhabited by Armenians, which
the Danishmend Turks were engaged in besieging. At their
approach, the Turks vanished; and though Bohemond set out
to pursue them he could not establish contact. The citizens
gladly welcomed their rescuers; who invited Taticius to
nominate a governor to rule the city in the Emperor's name.
Taticius gave the post to Peter of Aulps, a Provençal knight
who had first come to the east with Guiscard and then had
entered the service of the Emperor. It was a tactful choice; and
the episode showed that the Franks and Byzantines were still
able to cooperate and to carry out together the treaty made
between the princes and the Emperor.

From Comana the army advanced southeast to Coxon, the
modern Güksün, a prosperous town full of Armenians, set in a
fertile valley below the Anti-Taurus range. There it remained
for three days. The inhabitants were very friendly; and the
Crusaders were able to secure plentiful provisions for the next
stage of their march, across the mountains. A rumour now
reached the army that the Turks had abandoned Antioch.
Bohemond was still absent, pursuing the Danishmends; so
Raymond of Toulouse at once, without consulting more than
his own staff, sent five hundred knights under Peter of Castillon
to hurry ahead and occupy the city. The knights travelled at
full speed; but as they reached a castle held by Paulician
heretics not far from the Orontes, they learnt that it was a false
rumour and that on the contrary the Turks were pouring in
reinforcements. Peter of Castillon apparently rode back to
rejoin the army; but one of his knights, Peter of Roaix, slipped
away with a few comrades, and, after a skirmish with the Turks
of the locality, took over some forts and villages in the valley of
Rusia, towards Aleppo, with the glad help of the local
Armenians. Raymond's manoeuvre may not have been
intended to secure the lordship of Antioch for himself but only
the glory and the loot that would accrue to the first-comer. But
Bohemond, when he returned to the army, learnt of it with

suspicion; and it showed the growing breach between the princes.

The journey on from Coxon was the most difficult that the Crusaders had to face. It was now early October, and the autumn rains had begun. The road over the Anti-Taurus was in appalling disrepair; and for miles there was only a muddy path leading up steep inclines and skirting precipices. Horse after horse slipped and fell over the edge; whole lines of baggage animals, roped together, dragged each other down into the abyss. No one dared to ride. The knights, struggling on foot under their heavy accoutrement, eagerly tried to sell their arms to more lightly equipped men, or threw them away in despair. The mountains seemed accursed. They took more lives than ever the Turks had done. It was with joy that the army emerged at last into the valley that surrounded Marash.

At Marash, where again they found a friendly Armenian population, the Crusaders waited for a few days. An Armenian prince called Thatoul, who had been formerly a Byzantine official, was ruler of the town and was confirmed in his authority. Bohemond rejoined them there, after his fruitless pursuit of the Turks; and Baldwin came hurrying up from Cilicia, to see his wife Godvere, who was dying. After her death he departed again, making now for the east. Leaving Marash about 15 October, the main army marched, strengthened and refreshed, down into the plain of Antioch. On the 20th it arrived at the Iron Bridge, at three hours' distance from the city.

Four months had passed since the Crusade had set out for Nicaea. For a large army, with a numerous following of non-combatants, travelling in the heat of summer over country that was mainly barren, always liable to be attacked by a formidable and swiftly moving enemy, the achievement was remarkable. The Crusaders were helped by their faith and by their burning desire to reach the Holy Land. The hope of finding plunder and perhaps a lordship was an added spur. But some credit too must be given to the Byzantines that accompanied the expedition, whose experience in fighting the Turks enabled them to give good advice, and without whose guidance the route across Asia

Minor could never have been traced. The guides may have made some errors, as in the choice of their road from Coxon to Marash; but, after twenty years of neglect and occasional deliberate destruction, it was impossible to tell in what state any road might be. Taticius had a difficult part to play; but, till the army reached Antioch, his relations with the western princes remained friendly. The humbler Crusading soldiery might be distrustful of the Greeks; but, in so far as the direction of the movement was concerned, everything still ran smoothly.

Meanwhile the Emperor Alexius, who was to be responsible for the maintenance of communications across Asia Minor, was consolidating the Christian position in the rear of the Crusade. The success of the Franks had reconciled the Seldjuks with the Danishmends, thus creating, as soon as the shock of the first defeat was over, a strong potential Turkish force in the centre and east of the peninsula. The Emperor's policy was, therefore, to recover the west of the peninsula, where, with the aid of his growing maritime power, he could open up a road to the south coast which it would be possible to keep under his permanent control. After refortifying Nicaea and securing the fortresses commanding the road to Dorylaeum, he sent his brother-in-law, the Caesar John Ducas, supported by a squadron under the admiral Caspax, to reconquer Ionia and Phrygia. The main objective was Smyrna, where Chaka's son still ruled over an emirate that included most of the Ionian coastline and the islands of Lesbos, Chios and Samos, while vassal Emirs held Ephesus and other towns near the coast. Phrygia was under Seldjuk chieftains, now cut off from contact with the Sultan. To impress the Turks, John took with him the Sultana, Chaka's daughter, for whom arrangements had not yet been made to join her husband. The combined land and sea attack was too much for the Emir of Smyrna, who promptly surrendered his states in return for permission to retire free to the east. He seems to have escorted his sister to the Sultan's court, where he disappears from history. Ephesus fell next, with hardly a struggle; and while Caspax and his fleet reoccupied the coast and the islands, John Ducas marched inland, capturing one by one the chief Lydian cities, Sardis, Philadelphia and Laodicea.

The province was in his hands by the end of the autumn of
1097; and he was ready, as soon as the winter should be over,
to advance into Phrygia, as far as the main road down which
the Crusaders had travelled. His aim was probably to re-
establish Byzantine control of the road that led from Polybotus
and Philomelium due south to Attalia, and thence along the
coast eastward, where sea-power would give protection and
junction could be made with the Armenian princes that were
now settled in the Taurus mountains. A route would thus be
ensured by which supplies could reach the Christians battling
in Syria, and the united effort of Christendom could continue.

CHAPTER 10

Armenian interlude

Trust ye not in a friend.

Micah VII, 5

The Armenian migration to the southwest, begun when the Seldjuk invasions made life in the Araxes valley and by Lake Van no longer secure, continued throughout the last years of the eleventh century. When the Crusaders arrived in eastern Asia Minor there was a series of small Armenian principalities stretching from beyond the middle Euphrates to the heart of the Taurus mountains. The ephemeral state that the Armenian Philaretus had founded had crumbled even before his death in 1090. But Thoros still held Edessa, where he had recently managed to eject the Turkish garrison from the citadel; and his father-in-law, Gabriel, still held Melitene. At Marash the leading Christian citizen, Thatoul, was recognized as governor by the Byzantine authorities to whom the Crusaders restored the town. At Raban and Kaisun, between Marash and the Euphrates, an Armenian called Kogh Vasil, Vasil the Robber, had set up a small principality. Thoros and Gabriel, and probably Thatoul also, had been lieutenants of Philaretus and like him had started their public careers in the Byzantine administrative service. Not only did they belong to the Orthodox Church, and not to the separated Armenian Church, but they continued to use the titles that they had received long ago from the Emperor; and, whenever possible, they re-established relations with the Court at Constantinople, re-affirming their allegiance. Thoros had, indeed, received from Alexius the high title of curopalates. This imperial connection gave to their government a certain legitimacy; but a more solid base was provided by their readiness to accept the suzerainty of neighbouring Turkish chieftains. Thoros played off these potential suzerains one against the other with surprising agility; while Gabriel had sent his wife on a mission to Baghdad to obtain recognition from the highest Moslem authorities. But all these princes were in a precarious position. With the exception of Kogh Vasil, they were separated by their religion from most of their compatriots and hated by the Syrian Christians who still were plentiful in their territories; and all were distrusted by the Turks, whose disunion alone enabled them to survive.

The Armenians in the Taurus were less exposed to danger; for the territory in which they were settled was hard of access and easy to defend. Oshin, son of Hethoum, now controlled the mountains to the west of the Cilician Gates, with his headquarters at the impregnable castle of Lampron on a high spur overlooking Tarsus and the Cilician plain. He kept up a fitful connection with Constantinople and had been given by the Emperor the title of stratopedarch of Cilicia. Though not, it seems, a member of the Orthodox Church, he had served under Alexius in the past; and it was probably with the Emperor's approval that he had taken over Lampron from its unconquered Byzantine garrison. He made frequent excursions into the Cilician plain; and in 1097 he took advantage of the Turkish pre-occupation with the advance of the Crusaders to capture part of the town of Adana. East of the Cilician Gates the mountains were in the possession of Constantine, son of Roupen, with his headquarters at the castle of Partzerpert, to the northwest of Sis. He had, since his father's death, extended his power eastward towards the Anti-Taurus and had captured the great castle of Vahka, on the Göksü river, from its isolated Byzantine garrison. He was a passionate adherent of the separated Armenian Church and, like his father, as heir of the Bagratid dynasty kept up a family feud against Byzantium. He, too, hoped to use the embarrassment of the Turks to establish himself in the rich Cilician plain, where already the population was largely Armenian.

Baldwin of Boulogne had for some time past interested himself in the Armenian question. At Nicaea he had struck up a close friendship with an Armenian, formerly in the Emperor's service, Bagrat, the brother of Kogh Vasil; and Bagrat had joined his staff. It is probable that Bagrat was anxious to secure Baldwin's help for the Armenian principalities near the Euphrates where his family connections lay. But when at Heraclea Tancred announced his intention of leaving the main army to try his fortune in Cilicia, Baldwin decided that it would be unwise to allow any other western prince to be the first to embark on an Armenian venture, if he was to reap the advantage of being the chief friend of that race. It is unlikely that he and Tancred had come to any understanding together. Both were junior members of a princely family, without any future at home; and both frankly wished to found lordships in the East. But while Baldwin had already decided upon an Armenian state, Tancred was ready to set himself up wherever it seemed most convenient. He opposed the detour to Caesarea because it was a Byzantine suggestion from which the Byzantines were to benefit; and the presence of a friendly Christian population close at hand offered him an opportunity.

About 15 September Tancred, with a small group of a hundred knights and two hundred infantrymen, left the Crusader camp at Heraclea and made straight for the Cilician Gates. Immediately afterwards Baldwin set out, with his cousin Baldwin of Le Bourg, Rainald of Toul and Peter of Stenay and five hundred knights and two thousand infantrymen. Neither expedition burdened itself with non-combatants; and Baldwin's wife, Godvere, and her children remained with the main army. Tancred seems to have taken the direct road for the pass, travelling as the railway does today past Ulukishla; but Baldwin, with his heavier army, preferred the old main road which came down to Podandus, at the head of the pass, from Tyana, further to the east. He was therefore three days behind Tancred in going through the defile.

On descending into the plain, Tancred marched on Tarsus, which was still the chief city of Cilicia. Meanwhile he sent back to the main army to ask for reinforcements. Tarsus was held by a Turkish garrison, which at once made a sortie to drive off the invaders but was severely repulsed. The Christian inhabitants of the city, Armenians and Greeks, then made contact with Tancred and begged him to take possession of it. But the Turks held out till, three days later, Baldwin and his army came into sight. Then, finding themselves outnumbered, they waited till nightfall and fled under cover of the darkness. Next morning the Christians opened the gates to Tancred; and Baldwin arrived to see Tancred's banner waving from the towers. Tancred was unaccompanied by any Byzantine official and certainly had no intention of handing over any conquest that he might make to the Emperor. But in Baldwin he discovered a more dangerous competitor who was equally careless of the treaty made at Constantinople. Baldwin demanded that Tarsus should be transferred to his authority; and Tancred, furious but powerless in face of his rival's greater strength, was forced to agree. He withdrew his troops and marched eastward towards Adana.

Baldwin had hardly taken possession of Tarsus when three hundred Normans arrived before the city, having come from the main army to reinforce Tancred. Despite their supplication, he refused to allow them to enter inside the walls; and while they were encamped outside they were attacked at night by the former Turkish garrison, which was now roaming the countryside, and were massacred to a man. The episode shocked the Crusaders. Baldwin was blamed for their fate even by his own army; and his position might have been badly damaged had not news come of the unexpected appearance of a Christian fleet in the bay of Mersin, at the mouth of the river Cydnus, just below the city, under the command of Guynemer of Boulogne.

Guynemer was a professional pirate who had been astute enough to see that the Crusade would need naval help. Collecting a group of fellow pirates, Danes, Frisians and Flemings, he had sailed from the Netherlands in the late spring and, having reached Levantine waters, was seeking to make contact with the Crusaders. He retained a sentiment of loyalty for his home town. He was therefore delighted to find close at hand an army whose general was the brother of his Count. He sailed up the river to Tarsus and paid homage to Baldwin. In return Baldwin borrowed three hundred of his men to serve as

a garrison of the town and probably nominated Guynemer to
act as his lieutenant there while he himself prepared to march
on to the east.

Meanwhile Tancred had found Adana in a state of confusion.
Oshin of Lampron had recently raided the town and left a force
there that was disputing it with the Turks; while a Burgundian
knight called Welf, who had probably started with Baldwin's
army but had broken off to see what he could gain, had also
forced his way in and now held the citadel. On Tancred's
arrival the Turks withdrew; and Welf, who welcomed his
troops into the citadel, was confirmed in his possession of the
town. Oshin was probably only concerned in extracting his
own men from a risky adventure. He was grateful for Tancred's
intervention; but he urged him to go on to Mamistra, the
ancient Mopsuesta, where a wholly Armenian population was
longing for deliverance from the Turks. He was eager to see the
Franks pass on into the sphere of influence coveted by his rival,
Constantine the Roupenian.

Tancred reached Mamistra early in October. As at Adana,
the Turks fled on his appearance; and the Christians gladly led
him into the town. While he was there, Baldwin and his army
came up. Baldwin seems to have decided already that his future
principality would not be in Cilicia. Possibly the climate,
steamy and malarial in September, had deterred him. Possibly
he felt it to be too close to the Emperor's growing power. His
adviser Bagrat was urging him eastward, where the Armenians
were appealing for his help. He had at any rate damaged
Tancred's chances of founding a strong Cilician state. Now he
was on his way back to the main army, to consult with his
brother and his friends before embarking on a fresh campaign.
But Tancred was reasonably suspicious. He would not permit
Baldwin to enter into Mamistra but obliged him to camp on the
far side of the river Jihan. He was ready, however, to allow
victuals to be sent off to the camp from the town. But many of
the Normans, led by Tancred's brother-in-law, Richard of the
Principate, could not endure that Baldwin should go un-
punished for his crime at Tarsus. They persuaded Tancred to
join them in a surprise attack on his camp. It was an unwise

move. Baldwin's troops were too numerous and too strong for them and soon drove them back in disorder across the river. The unedifying conflict provoked a reaction; and Baldwin and Tancred allowed themselves to be reconciled. But the harm was done. It had become painfully clear that the Crusading princes were not prepared to cooperate for the good of Christendom when a chance arose for acquiring personal possessions; and the native Christians were quick to realize that their Frankish rescuers were only superficially moved by altruistic sentiment and to learn that their best advantage lay in the easy game of playing off one Frank against another.

After the reconciliation at Mamistra, Baldwin moved quickly on to rejoin the main army at Marash. News had reached him that Godvere was dying; and their children too, it seemed, were sick and did not long survive. Baldwin only remained a few days with his brothers and the other chiefs of the army. Then, when the main force set out southward to Antioch, he went off to the east, to try his fortune in the valley of the Euphrates and the lands beyond. A far smaller company travelled with him than had gone on the Cilician expedition. Maybe his popularity as a leader had not recovered from the events at Tarsus; maybe his brothers, anxious for the capture of Antioch, could not now spare troops for him. He had only a hundred horsemen; but his Armenian adviser, Bagrat, still was with him; and he added a new chaplain to his staff, the historian Fulcher of Chartres.

Tancred did not remain long at Mamistra after Baldwin's departure. Leaving a small garrison there, he turned southward round the head of the Gulf of Issus to Alexandretta. As he journeyed he sent envoys to Guynemer, whose headquarters were probably still at Tarsus, asking for his cooperation. Guynemer responded gladly and came with his fleet to join Tancred before Alexandretta. A combined assault gave them the town, which Tancred garrisoned. He then marched over the Amanus range through the Syrian Gates to unite with the Christian army before Antioch.

The Cilician adventure had done little good either to Baldwin or to Tancred. Neither had found it worth while to found a state there. The small Frankish garrisons left in the three Cilician towns, Guynemer's at Tarsus, Welf's at Adana and Tancred's at Mamistra, would not be able to withstand any serious attack. The dispersal of the Turkish garrisons had, however, been of some value to the Crusade as a whole in preventing the use of Cilicia as a base from which the Turks could launch a flank attack on the Franks during their operations at Antioch; while the capture of Alexandretta provided the Franks with a useful port through which supplies could pass. But the chief beneficiaries of the whole affair were the Armenian princes of the hills. The collapse of Turkish power in the plain enabled them slowly to penetrate its villages and towns and to lay the foundations of the Cilician kingdom of Little Armenia.

When Baldwin left the main army at Marash, it was about to start upon its southward march to Antioch; and at first Baldwin took a parallel road a few miles to the east, so as to protect its left flank. It was perhaps by promising to undertake this task that he had obtained permission again to separate from the army; and, indeed, he could justify his whole expedition for the protection that it would give to the Crusade; for the easiest road by which reinforcements from Khorassan could reach the Turks at Antioch lay through the territory that he intended to invade. Moreover, its rich lands might provide the Crusade with the supplies of food that it required.

At Ain-tab Baldwin turned sharply to the east. It is doubtful if he had any planned course of action beyond a general determination to found a principality upon the Euphrates, which might be of profit to himself and to the whole Crusading movement. The circumstances were favourable. He would not have to conquer the country from the infidel; for it was already in friendly Armenian hands. He was in touch with its Armenian princes. Through Bagrat he must have entered into relations with Bagrat's brother, Kogh Vasil, whose lordship lay due east from Marash. Gabriel of Melitene, in permanent danger from the Danishmend Turks, was probably appealing for Frankish aid; while Thoros of Edessa was certainly in communication with the Crusaders. Indeed, Baldwin's decision to leave Cilicia was said to have been due to a message that he or Bagrat received there from Thoros, inviting him urgently to Edessa. The Armenians had long hoped to obtain succour from the West. Twenty years before, when Pope Gregory VII was known to be contemplating an expedition to rescue eastern Christendom, an Armenian bishop had travelled to Rome to secure his interest. Western allies had always seemed more attractive to them, even to the princes that bore Byzantine titles, than anything that might increase their dependence upon the hated Empire. The presence of a Frankish army fighting victoriously for Christendom on their very borders offered them the opportunity, for which they had prayed, to establish their independence once and for all from both Turkish and Byzantine domination. They eagerly welcomed Baldwin and his men as liberators.

We know nowadays to distrust the hopeful word 'liberation'. The Armenians learnt the lesson before us. As Baldwin moved towards the river Euphrates, the Armenian population rose up to greet him. The Turkish garrisons that remained in the district either fled or were massacred by the Christians. The only Turkish lord of any importance in the neighbourhood, the Emir Balduk of Samosata, who controlled the road from Edessa to Melitene, attempted to organize resistance but could not take any offensive measures. Two local Armenian nobles, called by the Latins Fer and Nicusus, joined Baldwin with their small levies. During the early winter of 1097 Baldwin completed his conquest of the land up to the Euphrates, capturing the two chief fortresses, Ravendel and Turbessel, as the Latins adapted the Arabic names Ruwandan and Tel-Basheir. Ravendel, which commanded his communications with Antioch, he put under the governorship of his Armenian adviser, Bagrat; while the command of Turbessel, important for its proximity to the historic ford across the Euphrates at Carchemish, was given to the Armenian, Fer.

While Baldwin was still at Turbessel, probably about the new year, an embassy reached him from Edessa. Thoros was impatient for the arrival of the Franks, whom he now saw delaying on the west bank of the Euphrates. His position was always precarious; and he was alarmed by the news that

Kerbogha, the terrible Turkish Emir of Mosul, was collecting a huge army which was destined for the relief of Antioch, but which could easily mop up Edessa and the Armenian states on its way. But Baldwin was not going on to Edessa except on terms that suited him. Thoros had expected to use him as a mercenary, paying him with money and rich gifts; but it was clear now that Baldwin wanted more than that. The Edessene embassy at Turbessel was now empowered to offer more; Thoros would adopt Baldwin as his son and heir and would at once co-opt him as partner in the government of his lands. To Thoros, who was childless and ageing, it seemed the only solution. It was not what he would have chosen but, unpopular at home and threatened by his neighbours, he could not afford to choose. But the less short-sighted amongst the Armenians were disquieted. It was not for this that Bagrat had schooled Baldwin in Armenian affairs. Bagrat himself was the first to show his discontent. While the Franks were still at Turbessel, Fer, who doubtless wished to succeed Bagrat in Baldwin's confidence, reported that he was intriguing with the Turks. It is probable that his intrigues were only with his brother, Kogh Vasil, with whom he was consulting about the new menace to Armenian freedom. Perhaps he hoped, too, to make himself prince of Ravendel. But Baldwin was taking no risks. Troops were rushed to Ravendel to arrest Bagrat, who was brought before Baldwin and tortured to confess what he had done. He had little to confess and soon escaped, to take refuge in the mountains, protected by his brother, Kogh Vasil, till he too was driven to join him in the wilderness.

At the beginning of February 1098, Baldwin left Turbessel for Edessa. Only eighty knights were with him. The Turks of Samosata laid an ambush for him where he was expected to cross the Euphrates, probably at Birejik, but he eluded them, slipping over a ford further to the north. He arrived at Edessa on 6 February, and was received with the greatest enthusiasm both by Thoros and by the whole Christian population. Almost immediately Thoros formally adopted him as his son. The ceremony, following the usual ritual of the Armenians of the time, was better suited to the adoption of a child than of a grown man; for Baldwin was stripped to the waist, while Thoros put on a doubly wide shirt, which he passed over Baldwin's head; and the new father and son rubbed their bare breasts against each other. Baldwin then repeated the ceremony with the princess, Thoros's wife.

Once established as heir and co-regent of Edessa, Baldwin saw that his first task must be to destroy the Turkish emirate of Samosata, which could too easily interrupt his communications with the west. The Edessenes gladly supported his scheme for an expedition, as the Emir Balduk was the closest and most persistent of their enemies, continually raiding their flocks and fields and occasionally extracting tribute from the city itself. The Edessene militia accompanied Baldwin and his knights against Samosata, together with an Armenian princeling, Constantine of Gargar, who was vassal to Thoros. The expedition, which took place between 14 and 20 February, was not a success. The Edessenes were poor soldiers. They were surprised by the Turks and a thousand of them were slain; whereupon the army withdrew. But Baldwin captured and fortified a village called St John, close to the Emir's capital, and installed the greater number of his knights there, to control the movements of the Turks. As a result there was a decline in the number of Turkish raids; for which the Armenians rightly gave Baldwin the credit.

Soon after Baldwin's return to Edessa a conspiracy against Thoros began to be hatched in the city, with the support of Constantine of Gargar. To what extent Baldwin was involved can never be known. His friends denied it; but according to the testimony of the Armenian writer Matthew he was informed by the conspirators of their intention to dethrone Thoros in his favour. The people of Edessa had no love for Thoros nor any gratitude for the agility with which he had preserved the independence of their city. They disliked him for being a member of the Orthodox Church and a titular official of the Empire. He had not been able to protect their harvests nor their merchandise from raiders; and he had extorted high taxation from them. But, till Baldwin appeared, they could not afford to dispense with him. Now they had a more efficient protector. It needed therefore no prompting from the Franks to provoke a conspiracy; but it is hard to believe that the conspirators would have ventured to go far without securing the approval of the Franks. On Sunday, 7 March, the conspirators struck. They whipped up the populace to attack the houses in which Thoros's officials lived, then marched on the prince's palace in the citadel. Thoros was deserted by his troops; and his adopted son did not come to his rescue but merely advised him to surrender. Thoros agreed and asked only that he and his wife might be free to retire to her father at Melitene. Though Baldwin apparently guaranteed his life, Thoros was not allowed to go. Finding himself imprisoned in his palace, he attempted on the Tuesday to escape from a window but was captured and torn to pieces by the crowd. The fate of the princess, Baldwin's adoptive mother, is unknown. On Wednesday, 10 March, Baldwin was invited by the people of Edessa to assume the government.

Baldwin had achieved his ambition of obtaining a principality. Edessa was not, indeed, in the Holy Land; but a Frankish state on the middle Euphrates could be a valuable element of defence for any state that might be set up in Palestine. Baldwin could justify himself on the lines of broad Crusading policy. But he could not legally justify himself before all Christendom. Edessa, as a city that had belonged to the Emperor before the Turkish invasions, was covered by the oath that he had sworn at Constantinople. He had moreover acquired it by displacing and conniving at the murder of a governor who was, officially at least, a recognized servant of the Empire. But Baldwin had shown already in Cilicia that his oath meant nothing to him: while at Edessa Thoros himself was ready to barter away his rights without reference to his distant suzerain. But the episode was not unnoticed by Alexius, who reserved his rights till he should be in a position to enforce them.

Later Armenian historians, writing when it was clear that the Frankish domination had brought about the utter ruin of the Armenians of the Euphrates, were severe in their condemnation of Baldwin. But they were unjust. There is no moral excuse for Baldwin's treatment of Thoros, as the embarrassed attitude of the Latin chroniclers well shows. Thoros had behaved in a similar manner to the Turk Alphilag, whom he had invited to save him from the Danishmends three or four years before and had caused to be murdered; but he acted then to save his city and his people from infidel tyranny; nor had Alphilag adopted him as his son. It is true that adoption was a less serious thing in Armenian custom than in western law; but that cannot lessen Baldwin's moral guilt. But the Armenians should not blame him; for it was by Armenians that Thoros was actually murdered; and Baldwin was invited to take his place with the almost unanimous approval of their race. The Armenian princes whom the Crusaders were to eject and who alone distrusted the value of their aid were men who had served the Empire in olden days. They were disliked by their compatriots for their allegiance to the Emperor, and, still more, for having become members of the Orthodox Church. These former Byzantine officials such as Thoros and Gabriel alone had had sufficient experience in government to preserve the existence of Armenian independence on the Euphrates. But their ungrateful subjects, with their loathing of Byzantium, with their readiness to forgive in a Latin the heretical errors that damned a Greek eternally in their eyes, had only themselves to blame if their Frankish friends were to lure them to disaster.

For the moment all was rosy. Baldwin took the title of Count of Edessa and made it clear that he intended to rule alone. But his Frankish troops were few in number; he was forced to rely upon Armenians to work for him. He found several that he could trust; and his task was made easier by the discovery in the citadel of a vast store of treasure, much of which dated from the days of the Byzantines and to which Thoros by his exactions had greatly added. The new-gotten wealth enabled him not only to buy support but to carry off a master-stroke of diplomacy. The Emir Balduk of Samosata had been frightened by the news of Baldwin's accession. When he saw preparations being made for a fresh attack on his capital he hastily sent to Edessa offering to sell his emirate for the sum of ten thousand bezants. Baldwin accepted, and entered Samosata in triumph. In the citadel there he found many hostages that Balduk had taken from Edessa. He promptly restored them to their families. This action, together with his elimination of the Turkish menace from Samosata, enormously increased his popularity. Balduk was invited to take up residence at Edessa with his bodyguard, as mercenaries of the count.

As Baldwin's successes became generally known, several western knights, on their way to reinforce the Crusading army at Antioch, turned aside to share in his fortune, while others left the dreary siege of Antioch to join him. Amongst these were Drogo of Nesle and Rainald of Toul and Raymond's vassal, Gaston of Béarn. Baldwin rewarded them with handsome gifts from his treasury and, to settle them, encouraged them to marry Armenian heiresses. He himself, a widower and childless now, set the example. His new countess was the daughter of a chieftain known to the Latin chroniclers as Taphnuz or Tafroc. He was a wealthy prince owning territory nearby and apparently was related to Constantine of Gargar; and he had connections with Constantinople, whither he ultimately retired. It is possible that he was the same as Thatoul, the ruler of Marash, whose alliance would certainly be of value to Baldwin. He gave his daughter a dowry of sixty thousand bezants and a vague promise that she should inherit his lands. But the marriage brought her no happiness; and no children were born of it.

Baldwin thus laid down the principles of the policy that he was later to establish for the kingdom of Jerusalem. The control of the government was to be kept by the Frankish prince and his Frankish vassals; but Orientals, both Christian and Moslems, were invited to play their part in the state, which a general fusion of races would in the end blend into a corporate whole. It was the policy of a clear-sighted statesman; but to knights newly come from the West, pledged to dedicate themselves to the Cross and to extirpate the infidel, it seemed almost a betrayal of the vows of a Crusader. It was not to set up Baldwin and his like in semi-Oriental monarchies that Urban had appealed to the faithful at Clermont.

Nor was it at first an easy policy to follow. The Moslems regarded Baldwin as a transitory adventurer of whom use might be made. Between Edessa and the Euphrates, to the southwest of the city, lay the Moslem town of Saruj. It was tributary to an Ortoqid prince, Balak ibn Bahram, but had recently revolted. Balak now wrote to Baldwin asking to hire his services for its reduction; and Baldwin, delighted by the opportunity thus opened to him, agreed to perform the task. The citizens of Saruj thereupon sent secretly to Balduk to come and save them. Balduk and his troops slipped out of Edessa and were admitted to Saruj. But Baldwin followed on his heels, bringing with him a number of siege engines. Balduk and the men of Saruj lost heart. The latter at once offered to give up their town to him and to pay him tribute, while the former came out to meet him, declaring that he had hurried ahead merely to take over the town for him. Baldwin was undeceived. He accepted Balduk's apology and apparently restored him to favour; but a few days later he demanded that the Emir's wife and children should be handed to him as hostages. When Balduk demurred, he arrested him and cut off his head. Meanwhile a Frankish garrison was placed in Saruj, under Fulk of Chartres; who is not to be confused with the historian Fulcher. The episode taught Baldwin that the Moslems could not be trusted. Henceforward he saw to it that any of them dwelling in his territory should be leaderless; but he allowed them freedom of worship. If he was to hold a town like Saruj, where the population was almost entirely Arab and Moslem, he could not do otherwise. But his tolerance shocked western opinion.

The capture of Saruj, which was followed a few months later by that of Birejik, with its ford over the Euphrates, by clearing the roads between Edessa and his fortresses of Turbessel and Ravendel, consolidated Baldwin's county and ensured his communications with the main Crusade. At the same time it taught the Moslems that the Count of Edessa was a power to be taken seriously; and they concentrated on his destruction. Their determination and the value of a Frankish Edessa to the Crusades were illustrated in May, when Kerbogha, on his way to relieve Antioch, paused to eliminate Baldwin. For three weeks he battled vainly against the walls of Edessa before he abandoned the attack. His failure raised Baldwin's prestige; and the time that he had lost saved the Crusade.

The Armenians also had not taken Baldwin seriously enough. They resented the flow of Frankish knights into their territory, and the favours that Baldwin bestowed on them. Nor did the Frankish knights placate the Armenians, whom they treated with disdain and often with violence. The notables of Edessa found themselves excluded from the count's council where only Franks were represented; but the taxes that they paid were no lower than in Thoros's day. Moreover Armenian estates in the countryside were being granted to the newcomers; and the farmers were bound to them by the tighter feudal custom of the West. Late in 1098 an Armenian revealed to Baldwin a plot against his life. Twelve of the chief citizens of the town were said to have been in touch with the Turkish Emirs of the Diarbekir district. Baldwin's father-in-law, Taphnuz, was at Edessa at the time; his daughter's wedding had taken place only a short time before. It was said that the conspirators wished to put him in Baldwin's place or at least to oblige Baldwin to share the government with him. On hearing the report Baldwin struck at once. The two leading plotters were arrested and blinded; their chief associates had their noses or their feet cut off. A large number of Armenians suspected of complicity were flung into gaol and their fortunes were confiscated. But, after the manner of wise Orientals, they had hidden their money well enough for it to elude Baldwin's inspectors; so Baldwin graciously allowed them to buy their freedom at prices ranging from twenty to sixty thousand bezants a head. Taphnuz, whose association with the plot could not be proved, nevertheless thought it wise to hasten back to his mountains. He took with him most of the countess's dowry, of which he had only handed over seven hundred bezants.

Baldwin's fierce crushing of the conspiracy ended the risk of trouble from his Armenian subjects. He continued to employ a few of them in high posts, such as Abu'l Gharib, whom he made governor of Birejik. But as more Franks joined him, attracted by his renown, he could afford to ignore the Orientals. His renown was now, less than a year after his coming to Edessa, already tremendous. While the main Crusading army was still toiling on the way to Jerusalem, he had founded a rich and powerful state deep in Asia and was feared and respected throughout the eastern world. He had started out on the Crusade a youngest son, penniless and dependent on the charity of his brothers. He had been utterly overshadowed by great nobles such as Raymond of Toulouse or Hugh of Vermandois or by experienced adventurers such as Bohemond. Already he was a greater potentate than any of them. In him the Crusade could recognize the ablest and most astute of its statesmen.

Before the walls of Antioch

> Only the trees which thou knowest that they be not trees
> for meat, thou shalt destroy and cut them down; and thou
> shalt build bulwarks against the city that maketh war
> with thee, until it be subdued.

Deuteronomy xx, 20

The city of Antioch lies on the river Orontes, some twelve miles
from the sea. It was founded in the year 300 BC by Seleucus I
of Syria and called after his father. It soon rose to be the chief
city in Asia; and under the Roman Empire it was the third city
in the world. To the Christians it was especially holy; for there
they had first been given the name of Christian; and there
Saint Peter had founded his first bishopric. In the sixth century
AD earthquakes and a sack by the Persians had diminished its
splendour; and after the Arab conquest it had declined, to the
profit of its inland rival Aleppo. Its recovery by Byzantium in
the tenth century restored some of its greatness. It became the
chief meeting place of Greek and Moslem commerce and the
most formidable fortress on the Syrian frontier. Suleiman ibn
Kutulmish captured it in 1085. On his death it passed to the
Sultan Malik Shah, who installed as governor the Turcoman
Yaghi-Siyan. Yaghi-Siyan had now ruled the city for ten years.
Since Malik Shah's death his nominal suzerain had been the
Emir Ridwan of Aleppo; but he was an undutiful vassal and
preserved practical independence by playing off against
Ridwan his rivals Duqaq of Damascus and Kerbogha of Mosul.
In 1096 Yaghi-Siyan had even betrayed Ridwan during a war
against Duqaq whom he now called his overlord; but his aid

had not enabled Duqaq to take Aleppo, whose Emir never forgave him.

The news of the Christian advance alarmed Yaghi-Siyan. Antioch was the acknowledged objective of the Crusaders; and, indeed, they could not hope to be able to march southward towards Palestine unless the great fortress was in their hands. Yaghi-Siyan's subjects were most of them Christians, Greeks, Armenians and Syrians. The Syrian Christians, hating Greeks and Armenians alike, might remain loyal; but he could not trust the others. Hitherto it seems that he was tolerant towards the Christians. The Orthodox Patriarch, John the Oxite, was permitted to reside in the city, whose great churches had not been turned into mosques. But with the approach of the Crusade he began restrictive measures. The Patriarch, the head of the most important community in Antioch, was thrown into prison. Many leading Christians were ejected from the city; others fled. The Cathedral of St Peter was desecrated and became a stable for the Emir's horses. Some persecution was carried on in the villages outside the city; which had for a result the prompt massacre of the Turkish garrisons by the villagers as soon as the Crusaders were at hand.

Next Yaghi-Siyan searched for allies. Ridwan of Aleppo would do nothing to help him, in short-sighted revenge for his treachery the previous year. But Duqaq of Damascus, to whom Yaghi-Siyan's son, Shams ad-Daula, had gone personally to appeal, prepared an expedition for his rescue; and his *atabeg*, the Turcoman Toghtekin, and the Emir Janah ad-Daula of Homs, offered their support. Another envoy went to the court of Kerbogha, *atabeg* of Mosul. Kerbogha was now the leading prince in upper Mesopotamia and the Jezireh. He was wise enough to see the threat of the Crusade to the whole Moslem world; and he had long had his eye on Aleppo. If he could acquire Antioch, Ridwan would be encircled and in his power. He, too, prepared an army to rescue the city; and, behind him, the Sultans of Baghdad and Persia promised support. Meanwhile Yaghi-Siyan collected his own considerable forces within the fortress and began to supply it with provisions against a long blockade.

The Crusaders entered Yaghi-Siyan's territory at the small town of Marata, the Turkish garrison fleeing at their approach. From Marata a detachment under Robert of Flanders went off to the southwest to liberate the town of Artah, whose Christian population had massacred the garrison. Meanwhile, on 20 October, the main army reached the Orontes at the Iron Bridge, where the roads from Marash and Aleppo united to cross the river. The bridge was heavily fortified, with two towers flanking its entrance. But the Crusaders attacked it at once, the Bishop of Le Puy directing the operations, and after a sharp struggle forced their way across. The victory enabled them to capture a huge convoy of cattle, sheep and corn on its way to provision Yaghi-Siyan's army. The road now lay open to Antioch, whose citadel they could see in the distance. Next day Bohemond at the head of the vanguard arrived before the city walls; and the whole army followed close behind.

The Crusaders were filled with awe at the sight of the great city. The houses and bazaars of Antioch covered a plain nearly three miles long and a mile deep between the Orontes and Mount Silpius; and the villas and palaces of the wealthy dotted the hillside. Round it all rose the huge fortifications constructed by Justinian and repaired only a century ago by the Byzantines with the latest devices of their technical skill. To the north the walls rose out of the low marshy ground along the river, but to the east and west they climbed steeply up the slopes of the mountain, and to the south they ran along the summit of the ridge, carried audaciously across the chasm through which the torrent called Onopnicles broke its way into the plain, and over a narrow postern called the Iron Gate, and culminated in the superb citadel a thousand feet above the town. Four hundred towers rose from them, spaced so as to bring every yard of them within bowshot. At the northeast corner the Gate of St Paul admitted the road from the Iron Bridge and Aleppo. At the northwest corner the Gate of St George admitted the road from Lattakieh and the Lebanese coast. The roads to Alexandretta and the port of St Symeon, the modern Suadiye, left the city through a great gate on the riverbank and across a fortified bridge. Smaller gates, the Gate of the Duke and the Gate of the

Dog, led to the river further to the east. Inside the enceinte water was abundant; there were market-gardens and rough pasture ground for flocks. A whole army could be housed there and provisioned against a long siege. Nor was it possible entirely to surround the city; for no troops could be stationed on the wild precipitous terrain to the south.

It was only through treachery that the Turks had taken Antioch in 1085; and treachery was the only danger that Yaghi-Siyan had to face. But he was nervous. If the Crusaders were not able to encircle the city, he on his side had not enough soldiers to man all its walls. Till reinforcements came up he could not risk losing any of his men. He made no attempt to attack the Crusaders as they moved up into position, and for a fortnight he left them unmolested.

On their arrival the Crusaders installed themselves outside the northeast corner of the walls. Bohemond occupied the sector opposite the Gate of St Paul, Raymond that opposite the Gate of the Dog, with Godfrey on his right, opposite the Gate of the Duke. The remaining armies waited behind Bohemond, ready to move up where they might be required. The Bridge Gate and the Gate of St George were for the moment left uncovered. But work was at once started on a bridge of boats to cross the river from Godfrey's camp to the village of Talenki, where the Moslem cemetery lay. This bridge enabled the army to reach the roads to Alexandretta and St Symeon; and a camp was soon established on the north of the river.

Yaghi-Siyan had expected an immediate assault on the city. But, amongst the Crusading leaders, only Raymond advised that they should try to storm the walls. God, he said, who had protected them so far, would surely give them the victory. His faith was not shared by the others. The fortifications daunted them; their troops were tired; they could not afford heavy losses now. Moreover, if they delayed, reinforcements would join them. Tancred was due to arrive from Alexandretta. Perhaps the Emperor would soon come with his admirable siege engines. Guynemer's fleet might spare them men; and there were rumours of a Genoese fleet in the offing. Bohemond, whose counsel carried most weight among them, had his private reasons for opposing Raymond's suggestion. His ambitions were now centred on the possession of Antioch for himself. Not only would he prefer not to see it looted by the rapacity of an army eager for the pleasure of looting a rich city; but, more seriously, he feared that were it captured by the united effort of the Crusade he could never establish an exclusive claim to it. He had learnt the lesson taught by Alexius at Nicaea. If he could arrange for its surrender to himself, his title would be far harder to dispute. In a little time he should be able to make such an arrangement; for he had some knowledge of Oriental methods of treachery. Under his influence Raymond's advice was ignored; Raymond's hatred of him grew greater; and the one chance of quickly capturing Antioch was lost. For, had the first attack met with any success, Yaghi-Siyan, whose nerve was shaking, would have put up a poor resistance. The delay restored his confidence.

Bohemond and his friends had no difficulty in finding intermediaries through whom they could make connections with the enemy. The Christian refugees and exiles from the city kept close touch with their relatives within the walls, owing to the gaps in both blockade and the defence. The Crusaders were well informed of all that passed inside Antioch. But the system worked both ways; for many of the local Christians, in particular the Syrians, doubted whether Byzantine or Frankish rule was preferable to Turkish. They were prepared to ingratiate themselves with Yaghi-Siyan by keeping him equally well informed of all that went on in the Crusaders' camp. From them he learnt of the Crusaders' reluctance to attack. He began to organize sorties. His men would creep out from the western gate and cut off any small band of foraging Franks that they could find separated from the army. He communicated with his garrison out at Harenc, across the Iron Bridge on the road to Aleppo, and encouraged it to harass the Franks in the rear. Meanwhile he heard that his son's mission to Damascus had succeeded and that an army was coming to relieve him.

As autumn turned to winter, the Crusaders, who had been unduly cheered by Yaghi-Siyan's preliminary inaction, began to lose heart, despite some minor successes. In the middle of

November an expedition led by Bohemond managed to lure the garrison of Harenc from their fortress and to exterminate it completely. Almost the same day a Genoese squadron of thirteen vessels appeared at the port of St Symeon, which the Crusaders were thereupon able to occupy. It brought reinforcements in men and armaments, in belated response to Pope Urban's appeal to the city of Genoa, made nearly two years before. Its arrival gave the Crusaders the comfortable knowledge that they now could communicate by sea with their homes. But these successes were overshadowed by the problem of feeding the army. When the Crusaders had first entered the plain of Antioch, they had found it full of provisions. Sheep and cattle were plentiful, and the village granaries still contained most of the year's harvest. They had fed well and neglected to lay in supplies for the winter months. Troops were now obliged to go foraging over an ever larger radius, and were all the more liable to be cut off by Turks coming down from the mountains. It was soon discovered that the raiders from Antioch would creep through the gorge of the Onopnicles and wait on the hill above Bohemond's camp to attack stragglers returning late to their quarters. To counter this, the leaders decided to build a fortified tower on the hill, which each of them guaranteed to garrison in turn. The tower was soon constructed and named Malregard.

About Christmas time 1097, the army's stocks of food were almost exhausted; and there was nothing more to be obtained in the neighbouring countryside. The princes held a council at which it was decided that a portion of the army should be sent under Bohemond and Robert of Flanders up the Orontes valley towards Hama, to raid the villages there and carry off all the provisions on which they could lay hands. The conduct of the siege should be meantime left in the hands of Raymond and the Bishop of Le Puy. Godfrey at the time was seriously ill. Bohemond and Robert set out on 28 December, taking with them some twenty thousand men. Their departure was at once known to Yaghi-Siyan. He waited till they were well away, then, on the night of the 29th, made a sortie in strength across the bridge and fell on the Crusaders encamped north of the

river. These were probably Raymond's troops, who had moved
from their first station when the winter rains made the low
ground between the river and the walls no longer habitable.
The attack was unexpected; but Raymond's alertness saved the
situation. He hastily collected a group of knights and charged
out of the darkness on the Turks; who turned and fled back
across the bridge. So hotly did Raymond pursue them that for
a moment his men obtained a foothold across the bridge before
the gates could be swung shut. It seemed that Raymond was
about to justify his belief that the city could be stormed, when
a horse that had thrown its rider suddenly bolted back, pushing
the knights crowded on the bridge into confusion. It was too
dark to see what was happening; and a panic arose among the
Crusaders. In their turn they fled, pursued by the Turks, till
they rallied at their camp by the bridge of boats; and the Turks
returned to the city. Many lives were lost on both sides, but
especially among the Frankish knights, whom the Crusade ill
could spare. Among them was Adhemar's own standard-
bearer.

Meantime Bohemond was riding with Robert of Flanders
southward, totally ignorant of how nearly Antioch had fallen to
his rival, Raymond, and ignorant, too, that a great Moslem
relief force was moving up towards him. Duqaq of Damascus
had left his capital, with his *atabeg* Toghtekin and with Yaghi-
Siyan's son Shams and a considerable army, about the middle
of the month. At Hama the Emir joined them with his forces.
On 30 December they were at Shaizar, where they learnt that
a Crusading army was close by. They marched on at once and
next morning came upon the enemy at the village of Albara.
The Crusaders were taken by surprise; and Robert, whose
army was a little ahead of Bohemond's, was all but surrounded.
But Bohemond, seeing what was happening, kept the bulk of
his troops in reserve, to charge upon the Moslems at the
moment when they thought that the battle was won. His
intervention saved Robert and inflicted such heavy losses on
the Damascene army that it fell back on Hama. But the
Crusaders, though they claimed the victory and had indeed
prevented the relief of Antioch, were themselves too seriously

weakened to continue their foraging. After sacking one or two villages and burning a mosque, they returned, almost empty-handed, to the camp before Antioch.

They found their comrades deep in gloom. The disastrous battle on the night of the 29th had been followed next day by a severe earth-tremor, which was felt even at Edessa; and that evening the aurora borealis illuminated the sky. During the next weeks torrential rain poured down incessantly, and it grew steadily colder. Stephen of Blois could not understand why anyone complained of excessive sunshine in Syria. It was clear that God was displeased with His warriors, for their pride, their luxuriousness and their brigandage. Adhemar of Le Puy ordered a solemn fast for three days; but with famine already approaching the fast made little difference; and now the failure of the foraging expedition would mean starvation for many. Soon one man in every seven was dying of hunger. Envoys in search of food were sent as far as the Taurus mountains, where the Roupenian princes consented to provide what they could. Some supplies came from the Armenian monks settled out on the Amanus mountains; while local Christians, Armenian and Syrian, collected everything edible that they could find and brought it to the camp. But their motive was not philanthropy but gain. For one donkey-load of provisions eight bezants were charged; and these were prices that only the wealthiest soldiers could afford. The horses suffered even worse than the men, till only some seven hundred were left with the army.

A more generous helper was found in the island of Cyprus. The Bishop of Le Puy, acting no doubt on Pope Urban's instructions, had been assiduously establishing good relations with the Orthodox Church dignitaries of the East; whom he treated with a respect that belies the theory that the Pope envisaged the Crusade as a means for bringing them under his control. For the Patriarch of Antioch, imprisoned within the city, this friendship was as yet of little value; for the Turks would from time to time put him in a cage and hang him over the walls. But the Patriarch Symeon of Jerusalem, who had retired from his see when Ortoq's death made life there too insecure, was now in Cyprus. As soon as communications were opened, Adhemar made contact with him. Symeon was no friend of Latin usages, against which he had published a firm but moderate treatise; but he was glad to cooperate with the western Church for the good of Christendom. Already in October he had joined with Adhemar in sending a report on the Crusade to the Christians of the West. Now, hearing of the plight of the army, he regularly dispatched across to it all the food and wine that the island could spare.

The Patriarch's food parcels, plentiful though they were, could do little to alleviate the general misery. Pressed by hunger, men began to desert from camp to seek refuge in richer districts or to attempt the long road home. At first the deserters were obscure private soldiers; but one January morning it was found that Peter the Hermit himself had fled, accompanied by William the Carpenter. William was an adventurer with no desire to waste his time on a hopeless Crusade; he had already deserted an expedition in Spain; but why Peter should have lost his nerve is hard to understand. The refugees were pursued by Tancred and brought back in ignominy. Peter, whose reputation it was advisable to preserve, was pardoned in silence; but William was kept standing all night in Bohemond's tent and in the morning received from him a harsh and menacing lecture. He swore that he would never leave the army again till it reached Jerusalem; but he later broke his oath. Peter's prestige inevitably suffered; but he was soon to be given a chance to redeem it.

With the army daily diminishing from famine and from flight, Adhemar considered that a strong appeal for reinforcements must be made to the West. To give it the utmost authority, he drafted it in the name of the Patriarch of Jerusalem, whose permission he had presumably secured. The language of the appeal is significant for the light that it throws on Adhemar's ecclesiastical policy. The Patriarch addresses all the faithful of the West as leader of the bishops now in the East, both Greek and Latin. He entitles himself 'Apostolic'; he takes it upon himself to excommunicate any Christian who fails in his Crusading vows. It is the language of an independent pontiff. Adhemar could never have put it into the mouth of one who was intended to be made subject to the Bishop of Rome.

Whatever Urban's ultimate plans might be for the government of the eastern Churches, his legate was not preaching papal supremacy. We do not know what response the Patriarch's letter evoked in the West.

While the Crusaders showed a proper respect for the hierarchs of eastern Orthodoxy, their relations with its lay overlord deteriorated. Early in February the Emperor's representative Taticius suddenly left the army. He had accompanied the Crusade from Nicaea with a small staff and a company mainly of guides and engineers, and had apparently been on good terms with its leaders. At Comana and at Coxon they had correctly handed over their conquests to him; and he in his reports paid generous tribute to their fighting qualities. Several explanations were given at the time for his departure; but there is no need to reject the story that he told on his return to Constantinople. According to him, Bohemond sent for him one day, when it was already known that the Turks were about to make another effort to relieve Antioch, and told him in strict confidence that the other leaders believed the Emperor to be responsible for encouraging the Turks and were plotting to revenge themselves by taking his life. Taticius allowed himself to be convinced. Indeed, the temper of the army at this moment was such that a scapegoat might well be desired. Besides, he believed that the Crusaders, weakened and demoralized by hunger, could not now hope to take the great fortress. His advice that it should be starved into surrender by the occupation of the castles that commanded its more distant approaches had been ignored. He therefore announced that he must return to imperial territory to arrange for a more satisfactory system of revictualment and took a ship at the port of St Symeon for Cyprus. To show that he intended to return, he left most of his staff behind with the army. But as soon as he was gone Bohemond's propagandists suggested that he had fled from cowardice in face of the coming Turkish attack, if not from actual treachery. When the Emperor's representative acted so dishonourably, surely the Crusade was freed from any obligation towards the Empire. That is to say, Antioch need not be restored to it.

Next, Bohemond put it about that he was himself contemplating his departure from the army. He could not much longer ignore his obligations at home. Hitherto he had played a leading part in all the military operations of the Crusade; and, as he calculated, the prospect of losing his aid at this critical juncture terrified the army. He therefore allowed it to be understood that if he were given the lordship of Antioch it would compensate him for any losses that he might suffer owing to his absence from Italy. His fellow princes were not taken in by these manoeuvres; but among the rank and file he won much sympathy.

Meanwhile the Turks were massing again for the relief of Antioch. When Duqaq failed to bring the aid that he had promised, Yaghi-Siyan turned again to his former suzerain, Ridwan of Aleppo. Ridwan by now regretted his own inaction that had permitted the Franks to penetrate to Antioch. When Yaghi-Siyan readmitted his suzerainty, he prepared to come to his rescue, assisted by his cousin, Soqman the Ortoqid, from Diarbekir, and by his father-in-law, the Emir of Hama. Early in February the allies reoccupied Harenc, where they assembled for their attack on the Crusaders' camp. On hearing the news, the Crusading princes held a council in Adhemar's tent, where Bohemond proposed that while the infantry should remain in the camp to contain any sortie from the city, the knights, of whom there were only seven hundred now fit for service, should make a surprise onslaught on the invading army. His advice was taken. On 8 February, at nightfall, the Frankish cavalry slipped out across the bridge of boats and took up its position between the river and the Lake of Antioch, from which it could fall on the Turks as they advanced to cross the Iron Bridge. At daybreak the Turkish army came in sight; and at once the first line of the Crusaders charged, before the Turkish archers could be formed into line. The charge could not break the mass of the Turks; and the knights withdrew, luring the enemy to their chosen battleground, where the lake on the left and the river on the right prevented the great numbers of the Turks from outflanking them. On this narrow terrain the knights charged again, this time in full force. Before their weight, the more lightly armed Turks broke and fled, spreading confusion in the packed lines behind them. Soon the whole of Ridwan's army was in full disorderly retreat back to Aleppo. As they passed through Harenc, its garrison joined the fugitives, leaving the town for the native Christians to hand back to the Crusaders.

While the cavalry were winning this spectacular victory, the infantry were fighting a harder battle. Yaghi-Siyan made a sortie in full strength against the camp; whose defenders were beginning to lose ground, when, in the afternoon, the triumphant knights were seen approaching. As they drew near Yaghi-Siyan understood that the army of relief was beaten. He called his men back within the walls.

The defeat of the second relieving army, though it raised the morale of the Crusaders, did nothing to improve their immediate situation. Food was still very short, though supplies were beginning to arrive at the port of St Symeon, coming largely from Cyprus, where the Patriarch Symeon, and probably also the unappreciated Taticius, collected all that was available. But the road down to the sea was perpetually raided by parties slipping out of the city, who ambushed the smaller convoys; while the city itself received provision through the still unguarded Gate of St George and across the fortified bridge. To control the bridge and so to make the passage to St Symeon safe, Raymond proposed to build a tower on the north bank close by. But the project was held back owing to the lack of materials and of masons. On 4 March a fleet manned by Englishmen and commanded by the exiled claimant to the throne, Edgar Atheling, sailed into St Symeon. It brought pilgrims from Italy, but had called on its way at Constantinople, where Edgar had joined it, placing himself under the orders of the Emperor. There it had been loaded with siege materials and mechanics, whose, arrival was very timely. The fact that they were provided by the Emperor was carefully disregarded by the Crusaders.

Hearing that the fleet had put in, Raymond and Bohemond set out together, neither trusting the other alone, to recruit as many fighting-men as possible from its passengers and to escort the mechanics and material up to the camp. On 6 March, as they were returning laden along the road from St Symeon, they were ambushed by a detachment from the garrison of the city. Their troops were taken by surprise and fled in panic, leaving their loads in the hands of the enemy. A few stragglers rushed into the camp and spread the rumour that both Raymond and Bohemond were killed. At the news Godfrey prepared to go out to rescue the defeated army, when the Turks made a sudden sortie from the city against the camp, to provide cover under which the ambushers, now heavy with booty, could reach the gates. Godfrey's men, already armed to set out along the road to the sea, were able to hold the attack till Raymond and Bohemond appeared unexpectedly with the remnant of their forces. Their arrival, weakened though they were, enabled Godfrey to drive the Turks back into the city. The princes then united to intercept the raiders as they returned. Their tactics were entirely successful. The raiders, handicapped by their loads, were outmanoeuvred and massacred as they struggled to reach the bridge; and the precious building materials were recovered. It was said that fifteen hundred Turks were slain, many of them drowned while trying to cross the river. Among the dead were nine Emirs. That evening members of the garrison crept out to bury the dead in the Moslem cemetery on the north bank of the river. The Crusaders saw them and left them in peace, but next morning they dug up the corpses for the sake of the gold and silver ornaments that they wore.

The result of the Crusaders' victory was to complete the blockade of Antioch. With the workmen and materials now provided the planned fortress was built to command the approach to the fortified bridge. It was built close to a mosque by the Moslem cemetery and was officially called the castle of La Mahomerie, from the old French word for 'mosque'. But when the leaders debated in whose charge the castle should be placed, Raymond, whose idea it was to erect it, claimed its control for himself; and it was usually known as the castle of Raymond. The building was finished by 19 March. It soon proved its value in preventing any access to the bridge-gate. But the Gate of St George was still open. To bring it too under control it was next resolved to build a castle on the site of an old convent on the hill that faced it. The construction was completed in April and the castle entrusted to Tancred, who was allowed the sum of three hundred marks for his expenses. Henceforward no convoys of food were able to reach the city, nor could its inhabitants send, as had been their custom hitherto, their flocks to pasture outside the walls. Individual raiders could still climb over the walls on Mount Silpius or through the narrow Iron Gate, but could no longer attempt an organized sortie. While the garrison began to suffer from hunger, the Crusaders' problem of commissariat was eased. The better weather as spring came on, the possibility of foraging without the risk of sudden Turkish attacks and the readiness of merchants that had hitherto sold their goods at high prices to the garrison to do business now with the camp made more provisions available and raised the morale of the Franks. Soon after his castle had been built Tancred had captured a huge consignment of food destined for Yaghi-Siyan and conveyed by Christian merchants, Syrian and Armenian. Such successes led the Crusaders to hope that Antioch might now be starved into surrender. But it must be done quickly, for the terrible Kerbogha of Mosul was gathering his forces.

While they were still at Constantinople the Emperor Alexius had advised the Crusaders to arrive at some sort of understanding with the Fatimids of Egypt. The Fatimids were uncompromising enemies to the Turks; they were tolerant towards their Christian subjects and had always been ready to treat with the Christian powers. The Crusaders probably had not followed this advice; but in the early spring an Egyptian embassy arrived at the camp before Antioch, sent by al-Afdal, the all-powerful vizier of the boy Caliph, al-Mustali. His proposal seems to have been that a division should be made of the Seldjuk empire; the Franks should take northern Syria and Egypt should take Palestine. Al-Afdal no doubt regarded the Crusaders merely as the mercenaries of the Emperor and assumed therefore that such a division, based on the state of affairs before the Turkish invasions, would be perfectly acceptable. The western princes received the ambassadors with cordiality, though they did not commit themselves to any specific arrangement. The Egyptians stayed for some weeks at the camp and returned home accompanied by a small Frankish embassy and laden with gifts, chiefly derived from the booty captured in the battle on 6 March. The negotiations taught the Crusaders the advantages that might emerge from intrigues with the Moslem powers. Laying aside their religious prejudices they next, on the news of Kerbogha's preparations, sent to Duqaq of Damascus, asking for his neutrality and declaring that they had no designs on his territory. Duqaq, who regarded his brother Ridwan of Aleppo as his chief enemy and saw that Ridwan had reverted to his former neutrality, did not acquiesce with their wishes.

Early in May it was known that Kerbogha was on the march. Besides his own troops, men had been provided by the Sultans of Baghdad and of Persia and from the Ortoqid princes of northern Mesopotamia; Duqaq was waiting to join him; and at Antioch Yaghi-Siyan, though hard pressed, was still holding out. Amongst the Crusaders tension grew. They knew that unless they captured the city first they would be crushed between the garrison and the huge relieving army. The Emperor Alexius was now campaigning in Asia Minor. A desperate appeal was sent to him to hurry to their rescue. Bohemond, determined to win Antioch for himself, had special cause for worry. If the Emperor arrived before Antioch fell or if Kerbogha were defeated only with the Emperor's help, then it would be impossible not to restore Antioch to the Empire. Most of the princes were prepared to give Bohemond the city; but Raymond of Toulouse, probably supported by the Bishop of Le Puy, would not agree. Raymond's motives have often been discussed. He, alone of the princes, was not bound by an explicit oath to the Emperor; but he had left Constantinople on good terms with the Emperor; he hated and suspected Bohemond as his chief rival for the military leadership of the Crusade; and both he and the legate may have considered that if the oath was invalid, the Church, of which Adhemar was the representative, should alone be able to allot territory. After some discussion and intrigue a compromise was reached. If Bohemond were the prince whose troops first entered the city, and if the Emperor never came, he should receive it for himself.

Even so, Raymond demurred, but Bohemond already had reason to be satisfied.

Kerbogha's own miscalculation gave the Crusade a breathing-space. He did not like to advance on Antioch leaving a Frankish army in Edessa in a position to threaten his right flank. He did not realize that Baldwin was too weak for offensive action but was too strong in his great fortress to be easily displaced. For the last three weeks of May he paused in front of Edessa, vainly attacking its walls, before he decided that the effort and the time lost were not worth while.

During these three precious weeks. Bohemond was hard at work. At some time he had established a connection with a captain inside the city of Antioch, whose name was Firouz. Firouz was apparently an Armenian converted to Islam, who had risen to a high position in Yaghi-Siyan's government. Though outwardly loyal he was jealous of his master, who had recently fined him for hoarding grain; and he kept in touch with his former co-religionists. Through them he reached an understanding with Bohemond and agreed to sell the city. The secret of the transaction was well kept. Bohemond took no one into his confidence. Instead, he publicly emphasized the dangers ahead in order to increase the value of his coming triumph.

His propaganda was only too successful. At the end of May Kerbogha abandoned the profitless siege of Edessa and continued his advance. As he approached, panic began to spread in the Crusaders' camp. Deserters began to slip away in such numbers that it was useless to try to stop them. At last, on 2 June, a large body of the northern French took the road to Alexandretta, led by Stephen of Blois. Only two months before Stephen had written cheerfully to his wife from the camp, to tell her of the difficulties of the siege but also to describe the triumphant battle of 6 March and to emphasize his own importance in the army. But now, with the city still untaken and Kerbogha's host at hand, it seemed to him mere folly to await for certain massacre. He had never been a great fighting man, but at least he would live to fight another day. Of all the princes Stephen had been most enthusiastic in his admiration for the Emperor. Bohemond must have smiled to see him go; but he could not foretell how useful his flight would be to his cause.

Had Stephen delayed his departure for only a few hours he would have changed his mind. On that very day Firouz sent his son to Bohemond to say that he was ready for the act of treachery. It was later rumoured that he had been hesitating right up till the evening before, when he discovered that his wife was compromised with one of his Turkish colleagues. He was now in command of the Tower of the Two Sisters and the adjoining section of the wall of the city on the outside, facing the castle of Tancred. He therefore urged Bohemond to assemble the Crusading army that afternoon and lead it out eastward, as though he were going to intercept Kerbogha; then, after dark, the troops should creep back to the western wall, bringing their ladders to scale the tower where he would be watching for them. If Bohemond agreed to this, he would send back his son as a hostage that evening as a sign that he was prepared.

Bohemond took his advice. As the day drew on he sent one of his infantrymen, whose name was Male Couronne, round the camp as a herald to bid the army be ready to set out at sunset for a raid in enemy territory. Then he invited the chief princes to see him, Adhemar, Raymond, Godfrey and Robert of Flanders, and, for the first time, told them of his plot. 'Tonight,' he said, 'if God favours us, Antioch will be given into our hands.' Whatever jealousy Raymond may have felt was left unspoken. He and his colleagues gave their loyal support to the scheme.

As the sun set the Crusading army set out eastward, the cavalry riding up the valley in front of the city and the infantry toiling over the hillpaths behind it. The Turks within the city saw them go and relaxed, in expectation of a quiet night. But in the middle of the night orders were given throughout the army to turn back to the west and northwest walls. Just before dawn Bohemond's troops arrived before the Tower of the Two Sisters. A ladder was placed against the tower; and, one after the other, sixty knights climbed up, led by Fulk of Chartres, and entered through a window high on the wall into a room where Firouz was nervously waiting. As they first entered he thought their numbers insufficient. 'We have so few Franks,' he cried out in Greek, 'where is Bohemond?' He need not have worried. From the Two Sisters the knights took over the other two towers under his control, enabling their friends to set ladders against the intervening stretches of the wall, while an Italian infantryman went to tell Bohemond that it was time for him to climb into the city. The ladder broke behind him; but while some of the soldiers ran along the wall, surprising the garrisons in their towers, others descended into the city and roused the Christian inhabitants and with their help flung open the Gate of St George and the great Gate of the Bridge, across which the bulk of the army was waiting. The Crusaders now poured in through the gates, meeting with little opposition. Greeks and Armenians joined them in massacring all the Turks that they saw, women as well as men, including Firouz's own brother. Many Christians perished in the confusion. Yaghi-Siyan himself, awakening to the clamour, at once concluded that all was lost. With his bodyguard he fled on horseback up the gorge that led to the Iron Gate and out on the hillside. But his son Shams ad-Daula kept his head. Gathering what men he could find he made his way up to the citadel before the Franks could overtake him. Bohemond followed but failed to force an entrance; so he planted his purple banner on the highest point that he could reach. The sight of it, waving in the light of the rising sun, cheered the Crusaders far below as they entered into the city.

When he had gathered enough men Bohemond attempted a serious assault on the citadel. But he was driven back and was himself wounded. His men preferred to return to the more agreeable task of sacking and looting the city streets; while he was soon consoled by receiving from an Armenian peasant the head of Yaghi-Siyan. Yaghi-Siyan had been thrown from his horse on a mountain path as he fled. His escort had deserted him; and as he lay there exhausted and half-stunned some Armenians had found him and recognized him. They killed him at once; and while one earned a handsome reward by bringing Bohemond his head the others sold his belt and his scimitar-sheath for sixty bezants apiece.

By nightfall on 3 June there was no Turk left alive in Antioch; and even from neighbouring villages to which the Franks had never penetrated the Turkish population had fled, to seek refuge with Kerbogha. The houses of the citizens of Antioch, of Christians as well as of Moslems, were pillaged. The treasures and the arms found there were scattered or wantonly destroyed. You could not walk on the streets without treading on corpses, all of them rotting rapidly in the summer heat. But Antioch was Christian once more.

CHAPTER 12

The possession of Antioch

He hath put forth his hands against such as be at peace with him: he hath broken his covenant.

Psalms LV, 20

The capture of Antioch was an achievement that gladdened Christian hearts. But when their triumphant frenzy died down and the Crusaders took stock of their position, they found themselves little better off than before. Great advantages had been gained. They had the city fortifications, undamaged in the battle, to protect them from Kerbogha's hosts; their civilian followers, numerous still in spite of disease and desertion, were sheltered and no longer the liability that they had been in the camp. The Turkish army that the city had contained was almost annihilated and no longer a steady threat. But the defence of the long line of the walls needed more men than they could now afford. The citadel was untaken and must be picketed. Though its garrison was too weak to take the offensive, from its summit every movement in the city could be watched; and it was impossible to prevent it from establishing a liaison with Kerbogha. In the city the Crusaders found none of the stores of food that they had hoped for, and themselves in their intoxication had destroyed most of its wealth. And though the Moslems were slain the native Christian population could not be trusted. The Syrians, in particular, had been treacherous in the past and had little sympathy for the Latins. Their treachery provided a far greater risk to an army defending the city than to one encamped outside. Moreover, the victory brought to a head a question that already showed signs of splitting the Crusade: to whom should the city be given?

At first there was no time to spare to debate the city's future. Kerbogha was advancing; and it must be defended against this present attack. Bohemond, whatever he might be planning, had not the troops to man the walls without the help of his colleagues. All must share in the defences; and each of the princes took over a section of the fortifications. The army's immediate task was to clear up the city and to bury the dead quickly, before the decaying corpses started an epidemic. While the soldiers were thus engaged, the Bishop of Le Puy arranged for the Cathedral of St Peter and the other churches that the Turks had desecrated to be cleaned and restored to Christian worship. The Patriarch John was released from his prison and replaced on the Patriarchal throne. John was a Greek, who disliked the Latin rite; but he was the legitimate Patriarch of a see still in full communion with Rome. Adhemar was certainly not going to offend against legitimacy and local sentiment by ignoring his rights. No one, aware of John's sufferings for the Faith, resented his restoration; except, perhaps, Bohemond, who may have foreseen its inconvenience to himself.

The Crusaders were barely able to instal themselves in the city before Kerbogha came up. On 5 June he reached the Orontes at the Iron Bridge; and two days later he encamped before the walls, on the very positions that the Franks had recently occupied. Shams ad-Daula at once sent envoys from the citadel to ask for his help. But Kerbogha insisted that the citadel should be taken over by his own troops. Shams begged to be allowed to retain command till the city should be retaken, but in vain. He was obliged to hand over the fortress and all its stores to Kerbogha's trusted lieutenant, Ahmed ibn Merwan.

Kerbogha's first plan was to penetrate into the city from the citadel. Foreseeing the danger, Bohemond and Raymond had constructed a rough wall to cut it off from the city fortifications. As it was the most vulnerable sector of the defence, it seems that the princes took turns to man it. After a little reconnoitring Ahmed ibn Merwan launched an assault on this sector, probably early on 9 June. Hugh of Vermandois, the Count of

Flanders and the Duke of Normandy were in charge of its defence, and were almost overpowered; but in the end they drove him back with heavy loss. After this Kerbogha decided that it would be less costly to blockade the Franks more closely and attack them later when they were weakened by starvation. On the 10th he moved in to encircle the city completely. The Crusaders sought to hinder him and made a fierce sortie but were soon forced to retreat again to the safety of the walls.

The failure of their effort cast the Crusaders into gloom. Their morale, raised for a while a week before by the capture of the city, sank now to its lowest depths. Food was again short. A small loaf cost a bezant, an egg two bezants and a chicken fifteen. Many men lived only on the leaves of trees or on dried hides. Adhemar of Le Puy vainly tried to organize relief for the poorer pilgrims. Amongst the knights there were many who thought that Stephen of Blois had chosen the wisest course. During the night of the 10th a company led by William and Aubrey of Grant-Mesnil and Lambert, Count of Clermont, managed to pass through the enemy lines and hurried down to the sea at St Symeon. There were Frankish ships in the harbour, probably some Genoese and some belonging to Guynemer's fleet. When the fugitives arrived and announced that the Crusading army was inevitably doomed, they hastily weighed anchor and set out for a safer port. The fugitives sailed with them for Tarsus. There they joined Stephen of Blois, who had planned to return to Antioch when he heard of its capture but had been deterred by a distant view of Kerbogha's army. William of Grant-Mesnil had married Bohemond's sister Mabilla; and the defection of so close a relative of the Norman chief could not fail to impress the army.

It seemed now to the men inside Antioch that their only chance of salvation would be the arrival of the Emperor and his forces. It was already known that Alexius had started out from Constantinople. During the spring John Ducas had advanced from Lydia into Phrygia as far as the main road down which the Crusaders had travelled and at some time had re-opened the road to Attalia. Alexius therefore judged it safe to take his main army on into the heart of Asia Minor in order to bring help to the Crusade, though many of his advisers disliked an expedition that would take him so far from his capital through country that was not yet cleared of the enemy. By the middle of June he was at Philomelium. While he was preparing to march on, Stephen and William appeared at the camp. They had sailed from Tarsus together, and on their journey, probably at Attalia, they heard of the Emperor's whereabouts. Leaving their men to go on by sea they hurried northward to Philomelium to tell him that the Turks by now were certainly in Antioch and the Crusader army annihilated. About the same time he was joined by Peter of Aulps, who had deserted his post at Comana, east of Caesarea, to report that a Turkish army was advancing to strike at Alexius before he could reach Antioch. Alexius had no reason to doubt their stories. Stephen had been a loyal and reliable friend in the past; and such a disaster was by no means improbable. The news forced him to reconsider his plans. If Antioch was taken and the Franks had perished, the Turks would certainly continue their offensive. The Seldjuks would undoubtedly attempt to regain what they had lost and they would have the whole victorious Turkish world behind them. Under such circumstances it would be madness to proceed with the expedition. As it was, his left flank was dangerously exposed to Turkish attacks. To lengthen his communications at this juncture, for a cause that was already lost, was unthinkable. Even had he been an adventurer such as the princes of the Crusade, the risk would hardly have been worth while. But he was responsible for the welfare of a great and vulnerable Empire; and his first duty was to his subjects. He summoned his council and told them that it was necessary to retire. There was a Norman prince on his staff, Bohemond's half-brother Guy, who had been for many years in his service. Guy was moved by the thought of the Crusaders' plight and begged the Emperor to march on, on the chance that they could still be saved. But no one supported his plea. The great Byzantine army retreated northward, leaving a cordon of waste land to protect the newly-won territory from the Turks.

It would have been well for the Empire and for the peace of eastern Christendom had Alexius listened to Guy's pleading;

though he could not have reached Antioch before the decisive battle had been fought. For when the rumour came to the Crusaders that the imperial army had turned back, their bitterness was intense. They saw themselves as the warriors of Christ against the infidel. To refuse to hurry to their aid, however hopeless it might seem, was an act of treason towards the Faith. They could not appreciate the Emperor's other duties. Instead, his neglect seemed to justify all the suspicion and dislike that they already felt for the Greeks. Byzantium was never forgiven; and Bohemond found it all to the profit of his ambition.

The Crusaders realized that Stephen of Blois was also to be blamed. Their chroniclers talked angrily of his cowardice; and the story soon reached Europe. He himself returned by easy stages home, to a wife who was furiously ashamed of him and who never rested till she had sent him out again to the East, to make atonement.

Meanwhile Kerbogha continued to press on Antioch. On 12 June a sudden attack almost gave him the possession of one of the towers on the southwest wall; which was preserved only by the bravery of three knights from Malines. To avoid the recurrence of such risks, Bohemond burnt down whole streets of the city near to the walls, thus enabling the troops to manoeuvre with greater ease.

At this juncture the spirits of the Christians were raised by a series of events which seemed to them to show God's special favour. The soldiers were hungry and anxious; the faith that had hitherto sustained them was wavering, but it was not broken. It was an atmosphere in which dreams and visions thrived. To the men of the Middle Ages the supernatural was not considered impossible nor even very rare. Modern ideas of the power of the subconscious were unknown. Dreams and visions came from God, or, in some cases, from the devil. Scepticism was confined to a flat disbelief in the word of the dreamer. This attitude must be remembered in considering the episode that follows.

On 10 June 1098, a poorly dressed peasant came to Count Raymond's tent and demanded to see him and the Bishop of Le

Puy. His name was Peter Bartholomew, and he had come on the Crusade as the servant of a Provençal pilgrim called William-Peter. He was not entirely illiterate, despite his humble origin, but he was known to his fellows as a rather disreputable character, interested only in the grosser pleasures of life. His story was that during the last months he had been tormented by visions in which Saint Andrew had revealed to him where one of the holiest relics in Christendom could be found, the Lance that had pierced the side of Christ. The first vision had occurred at the time of the earthquake of 30 December. He had been praying in terror when suddenly there appeared an old man with silver hair, accompanied by a tall and wonderfully beautiful youth. The old man, saying that he was Saint Andrew, bade him go at once to see the Bishop of Le Puy and Count Raymond. The Bishop was to be reproved for his neglect of his duties as a preacher; while to the Count was to be revealed the hiding-place of the Lance, which the saint now proposed to show to Peter Bartholomew. Peter then found himself borne, dressed as he was only in his shirt, to the interior of the city to the Cathedral of St Peter, which the Turks were keeping as a mosque. Saint Andrew led him in through the south entrance to the southern chapel. There he vanished into the ground to reappear carrying the Lance. Peter wished to take it at once but was told to return with twelve companions after the city was taken and to search for it in the same place. He was then wafted back to the camp.

Peter disregarded the saint's commands; for he feared that no one would listen to so poor a man. Instead, he went off on a foraging expedition to Edessa. At cock-crow on 10 February, when he was staying in a castle near Edessa, Saint Andrew and his companion appeared to him again, to reprove him for his disobedience, for which he was punished with a temporary malady of the eyes. Saint Andrew also lectured him about God's special protection of the Crusaders, adding that all the saints longed to resume their bodies to fight by their side. Peter Bartholomew admitted his guilt and returned to Antioch; but there his courage failed again. He did not dare accost the great princes, and was relieved when in March his master, William-

Peter, took him on a journey to buy food in Cyprus. On the eve
of Palm Sunday, 20 March, he was sleeping with William-Peter
in a tent at St Symeon, when the vision occurred once more.
Peter repeated his excuses; and Saint Andrew, after telling him
not to be afraid, gave instructions which Count Raymond was
to follow when he came to the river Jordan. William-Peter
heard the conversation but saw nothing. Peter Bartholomew
then returned to the camp at Antioch but was unable to obtain
an audience with the Count. He therefore left for Mamistra in
order to continue his journey to Cyprus. Saint Andrew came to
him there and angrily ordered him back. Peter wished to obey;
but his master made him embark to cross the sea. Three times
the boat was driven back and at last went ashore on an island
near St Symeon; where the journey was abandoned. Peter was
ill for a while; when he recovered Antioch had been captured;
and he entered the city. He took part in the battle on 10 June
and he narrowly escaped death from being crushed between
two horses; whereupon Saint Andrew made another appearance and spoke to him so sternly that he could no longer
disobey. He first told the story to his comrades. Despite the
scepticism with which it was received, he came now to repeat
it to Count Raymond and the Bishop of Le Puy.

Adhemar was not impressed. He considered Peter
Bartholomew to be a disreputable and unreliable character.
Possibly he resented the criticism of his own zeal as a preacher.
Possibly he remembered having seen at Constantinople a Holy
Lance whose claim of authenticity was longer established. As
an experienced churchman he distrusted the visions of the
ignorant. But Raymond, whose piety was simpler and more
enthusiastic, was ready to be convinced. He arranged to attend
at a solemn search for the Lance in five days' time. In the
meantime he confided Peter Bartholomew to the care of his
chaplain.

Visions breed rapidly. That evening all the princes were
gathered in the upper city, by the wall guarding the citadel,
when a priest from Valence called Stephen demanded to see
them. He told them that on the previous evening, believing
that the Turks had taken the city, he had gone with a group of

clerics to the Church of Our Lady to hold a service of intercession. At the end of it the others had fallen asleep; but as he lay wakeful there, he beheld before him a figure of marvellous beauty, who asked him who were these men and who seemed glad to learn that they were good Christians and not heretics. The visitor then asked Stephen if he recognized him. Stephen began to say No, but noticed a cruciform halo surrounding his head, as in the picture of Christ. The visitor admitted that he was Christ and next asked who was in command of the army. Stephen replied that there was no one commander but that the chief authority was given to a bishop. Christ then told Stephen to inform the bishop that his people had done evil with their lusts and fornication, but if they returned to a Christian way of life he would send them protection in five days' time. A lady with a brilliant countenance then appeared, saying to Christ that these were the people for whom she had so often interceded; and Saint Peter also joined them. Stephen tried to waken one of his comrades to bear witness to the vision; but before he succeeded the figures were gone.

Adhemar was prepared to accept this vision as genuine. Stephen was a reputable cleric and moreover swore on the Gospel that he had told the truth. Seeing that the princes were impressed with the story, Adhemar at once induced them to swear by the Holy Sacrament that none of them would henceforward leave Antioch without the consent of all the others. Bohemond swore the first, then Raymond, then Robert of Normandy, Godfrey and Robert of Flanders, followed by the lesser princes. The news of the oath raised the spirits of the army. Moreover Stephen's mention of a sign of divine favour due to come after five days gave support to Peter Bartholomew's claim. Expectation ran high in the camp.

On 14 June a meteor was seen which seemed to fall on to the Turkish camp. Next morning Peter Bartholomew was conducted to St Peter's Cathedral by a party of twelve, which included Count Raymond, the Bishop of Orange and the historian, Raymond of Aguilers. All day long workmen dug into the floor and found nothing. The Count went away in disappointment. At last Peter himself, clad only in a shirt, leapt into the trench. Bidding all present to pray, he triumphantly produced a piece iron. Raymond of Aguilers declared that he himself embraced it while it was still embedded in the ground. The story of its discovery soon spread round the army and was received with excitement and with joy.

It is useless to attempt now to judge what really happened. The cathedral had recently been cleaned on its reconsecration. Peter Bartholomew may have worked on the job after his return to Antioch, the date of which he never revealed, and would thus have had the chance of burying a piece of iron below the floor. Or he may have had the diviner's gift that can tell the presence of metal. It is remarkable that even in that age when miracles were universally considered to be possible, Adhemar clearly kept to the view that Peter was a charlatan; and, as the sequel was to show, this distrust was shared by many others. But it was not yet voiced. The finding of the relic had so heartened the Christians, even including the Greeks and Armenians, that no one wished to spoil its effect. Peter Bartholomew himself, however, somewhat shook his supporters two days later, when he announced another visit from Saint Andrew. Jealous, perhaps, of Stephen's direct conversation with Christ, he was pleased to hear from the saint that the silent companion in his visions was indeed Christ. Saint Andrew then gave him careful instructions of the services to be held in celebration of the discovery and on its anniversaries. The Bishop of Orange, made suspicious by all the liturgical detail, asked Peter if he could read. In reply Peter thought it wiser to declare that he was illiterate. This was shown to be a lie; but his friends were soon reassured; for thenceforward he was no longer able to read. Saint Andrew soon reappeared, to announce a forthcoming battle with the Turks that should not be long delayed, as the Crusaders were menaced with starvation. The saint recommended five fast-days, as a penance for the people's sins; then the army should attack the Turks, and it would be given the victory. There was to be no pillaging of the enemy's tents.

Bohemond, now in supreme command as Count Raymond was ill, had already decided that the only course was to launch a full assault on Kerbogha's camp; and it was possible that

Saint Andrew had been inspired from earthly sources in his latest advice. While the Crusaders' morale was improving, Kerbogha was finding increasing difficulty in keeping together his coalition. Ridwan of Aleppo still held aloof from the expedition; but Kerbogha now felt the need for his help. He began to negotiate with him, and thus offended Duqaq of Damascus. Duqaq was nervous about Egyptian aggression in Palestine and was anxious to return to the south. The Emir of Homs had a family feud with the Emir of Membij and would not cooperate with him. There was friction between the Turks and the Arabs in Kerbogha's own forces. Kerbogha himself attempted to maintain order by the use of autocratic authority which all the Emirs, who knew him to be a mere *atabeg*, resented. As the month went on there were more and more desertions from his camp. Large numbers of Turks and Arabs alike returned to their homes.

Kerbogha's difficulties were undoubtedly known to the Crusading leaders, who made an attempt to persuade him to abandon the siege. On 27 June they sent an embassy composed of Peter the Hermit and a Frank called Herluin, who spoke both Arabic and Persian, to his camp. The choice of Peter indicates that he had recovered from the disrepute caused by his attempted flight five months before. It was probably because they feared that the envoys' immunity would not be respected that none of the leaders could be allowed to go on the mission; and Peter was chosen as the best-known non-combatant with the army. His acceptance of the task showed courage and did much to restore his prestige. We do not know what terms Peter was empowered to offer; for the speeches put into his and Kerbogha's mouth by later chroniclers are clearly fictional. Possibly, as some of the chroniclers say, it was suggested that a series of single combats might decide the issue. Kerbogha, despite his growing weakness, still demanded unconditional surrender; and the embassy returned empty-handed. But in the course of it Herluin may have acquired some useful information about the state of affairs in the Turkish camp.

After the failure of the embassy there could be no alternative to battle. Early on Monday morning, 28 June, Bohemond drew up the Crusading troops for action. They were divided into six armies. The first was composed of the French and Flemish, led by Hugh of Vermandois and Robert of Flanders; the second of the Lotharingians, led by Godfrey; the third of the Normans of Normandy, under Duke Robert; the fourth of the Toulousans and the Provençals, under the Bishop of Le Puy, as Raymond was seriously ill; and the fifth and sixth of the Normans of Italy, under Bohemond and Tancred. To keep watch on the citadel, two hundred men were left in the city, for Raymond to command from his sickbed. While some of the priests and chaplains of the army held a service of intercession on the walls, others marched with the troops. To the historian Raymond of Aguilers was given the honour of carrying the Holy Lance into the battle. Each prince could be distinguished by his banner; but the panoply of the knights was a little tarnished. Many had lost their horses and had to go on foot or ride inferior beasts of burden. But, strengthened by the recent signs of divine favour, the soldiers' courage was high as they marched out, one after the other, across the fortified bridge.

As they emerged out of the gate, Kerbogha's Arab commander, Watthab ibn Mahmud, urged him to attack at once. But Kerbogha feared that to strike too soon would only destroy the Crusaders' advance-guard, whereas if he waited he might dispose of their whole forces in one stroke. In view of the temper of his troops he could not afford that the weary siege should go on. But when he saw the full array of the Franks he hesitated and sent a herald to announce, too late, that he would now discuss terms for a truce. Ignoring his messenger, the Franks advanced; and Kerbogha adopted the usual Turkish technique of retiring and luring them on into rougher ground, where suddenly his archers poured arrows into their ranks. Meanwhile he sent a detachment round to outflank them on the left, where they were unprotected by the river. But Bohemond was ready for this, and composed a seventh army, under Rainald of Toul, to hold this attack. On the main front the fighting was hard; among the slain was Adhemar's own standard bearer. But the Turkish archers could not stop the Crusaders' advance; and the Turkish line began to waver. The Christians pressed on, encouraged by a vision on the hillside of a company of knights on white horses, waving white banners, whose leaders they recognized as Saint George, Saint Mercury and Saint Demetrius. More practical aid was given them by the decision of many of Kerbogha's Emirs to desert his cause. They feared that victory would make him too powerful and they would be the first to pay for it. With Duqaq of Damascus at their head they began to leave the field; and their going spread panic. Kerbogha set fire to the dry grass in front of his line, in a vain attempt to delay the Franks while he restored order. Soqman the Ortoqid and the Emir of Homs were the last to remain faithful to him. When they too fled he saw that the game was up and abandoned the battle. The whole Turkish army broke up in panic. The Crusaders, following Saint Andrew's advice not to delay to sack the enemy camp, followed the fugitives as far as the Iron Bridge, slaying vast numbers of them. Others who tried to seek shelter in the castle of Tancred were rounded up and perished. Many of the survivors of the battle were massacred in their flight by the Syrians and Armenians of the countryside. Kerbogha himself reached Mosul with a remnant of his forces; but his power and prestige were lost for ever.

Ahmed ibn Merwan, the commander of the citadel, had watched the battle from his mountain top. When he saw that it was lost, he sent a herald to the city to announce his surrender. The herald was taken to Raymond's tent; and Raymond dispatched one of his own banners to be raised over the citadel-tower. But when Ahmed learnt that the banner was not Bohemond's, he refused to display it; for he had, it seems, already made a secret arrangement with Bohemond to be carried out in event of a Christian victory. He did not open his gates till Bohemond himself appeared, when the garrison was allowed to march out unharmed. Some of them, including Ahmed himself became converts to Christianity and joined Bohemond's army.

The Crusaders' victory was unexpected but complete. It decided that Antioch should remain in the possession of the Christians. But it did not decide to which of the Christians its possession would pass. The oath that all the princes except

Raymond had sworn to the Emperor clearly demanded that the city should be handed over to him. But Bohemond had already shown his intention to retain it; and his colleagues, with the exception of Raymond, were ready to consent, as it was he who had planned the capture of the city and he to whom the citadel had surrendered. They were a little uncomfortable at flouting their oaths. But the Emperor was far away. He had not come to their aid. Even his representative had left them; and they had taken the city and defeated Kerbogha without his help. It seemed to them impracticable to keep a garrison there till Alexius should deign to appear himself or send a lieutenant; and it seemed impolitic to waste time and to risk the enmity and perhaps the desertion of their most eminent soldier in defending the rights of an absentee. Godfrey of Lorraine clearly thought it foolish to stand in the way of Bohemond's ambitions. Raymond, however, was always bitterly jealous of Bohemond. And it would be unfair to regard his jealousy as his only motive in supporting the claims of Alexius. He had made friends with Alexius before he left Constantinople; and he was shrewd enough to see that by failing to restore Antioch to the Empire the Crusaders would forfeit the Emperor's goodwill, which was necessary for them if their communications were to be adequately maintained and if the inevitable Moslem counter-action was to be kept in check. The Crusade would no longer be an effort of united Christendom. Adhemar of Le Puy shared Raymond's point of view. He was determined to cooperate with the eastern Christians, as his master, Pope Urban, undoubtedly wished, and he saw the danger of offending Byzantium.

It was probably due to Adhemar's influence that Hugh of Vermandois was sent to explain the situation to Alexius. Now that Antioch was secure, Hugh wished to return home and to travel by way of Constantinople. The Crusaders still believed that Alexius was on his way across Asia Minor. News of his retreat after his interview with Stephen of Blois had not yet reached them. Adhemar and Raymond hoped that Hugh's mission would cause Alexius to hurry on to them. At the same time it was resolved that the Crusade should wait at Antioch till

1 November, before it attempted to march on to Jerusalem. It was a natural decision; for the army was tired, and to advance in the full heat of the Syrian summer, along little-known roads where water might be scarce, would be an act of folly. Moreover the question of Antioch must first be settled; and Adhemar doubtless hoped that the Emperor would have come by then. Hugh set out early in July, accompanied by Baldwin of Hainault. On the road through Asia Minor his party was attacked and severely mauled by the Turks. The Count of Hainault disappeared and his fate was never known. It was already autumn before Hugh arrived at Constantinople and could see the Emperor to tell him the full story of Antioch. By then the season was too late for a campaign across the Anatolian mountains. It was not feasible for Alexius to reach Antioch before the coming spring.

Meanwhile in Antioch tempers grew frayed. At first the citadel had been occupied jointly by Bohemond, Raymond, Godfrey and Robert of Flanders, but Bohemond retained the chief towers in his control. Now he succeeded in ejecting his colleagues' troops, probably with the consent of Godfrey and Robert, so that Raymond's objections were overruled. Raymond was furious, and in reply kept sole control of the fortified bridge and the palace of Yaghi-Siyan. But Raymond was still too ill to be active; and now Adhemar fell ill. With their two leaders in retirement, the southern French found themselves maltreated by the other troops, particularly by the Normans; and many of them longed for Raymond to be reconciled with Bohemond. Bohemond behaved as though he were already master of the city. Many Genoese had hastened to Antioch as soon as Kerbogha's defeat was known, eager to be the first to capture its trade. On 14 July Bohemond gave them a charter, allowing them a market, a church and thirty houses. Henceforward the Genoese would advocate his claims; and he could count on their assistance to keep open his communications with Italy. They agreed to support him in Antioch against all comers, except only the Count of Toulouse. In such a combat they would remain neutral.

While Raymond and Bohemond warily watched each other,

the lesser nobles rode off to join Baldwin at Edessa or made expeditions to capture plunder or even to set up fiefs in the country around. The most ambitious of these raids was conducted by a Limousin in Raymond's army, called Raymond Pilet, who set out on 17 July across the Orontes to the east, and three days later occupied the town of Tel-Mannas, whose Syrian population received him gladly. After capturing a Turkish castle in the neighbourhood he moved on to attack the larger town of Maarat an-Numan, with an army composed mainly of native Christians. But they were unused to bearing arms; and when they met the troops sent by Ridwan of Aleppo to save the town they turned and fled. But Ridwan was unable to eject Raymond Pilet from Tel-Mannas.

In the course of July a serious epidemic broke out in Antioch. We cannot tell its precise nature, but it was probably typhoid, due to the effect of the sieges and battles of the last month and the Crusaders' ignorance of the sanitary precautions necessary in the East. Adhemar of Le Puy, whose health had for some time been failing, was its first distinguished victim. He died on 1 August.

Adhemar's death was one of the greatest tragedies of the Crusade. In the chroniclers' pages he is rather a shadowy figure; but they show him to have wielded greater personal influence than any other Crusader. He commanded respect as the Pope's representative; and his own character won him the affection of the whole army. He was charitable and cared for the poor and the sick. He was modest and never aggressive; but he was always ready to give wise advice, even on military matters; as a general he was both courageous and shrewd. The victory at Dorylaeum had been largely due to his strategy; and he presided over many of the army councils during the siege of Antioch. Politically he worked for a good understanding with the Christians of the East, both with Byzantium and with the Orthodox churches of Syria. He had been in Pope Urban's confidence and knew his views. While he lived, the racial and religious intolerance of the Franks could be kept in check, and the selfish ambitions and quarrels of the princes restrained from doing irreparable harm to the Crusade. Though he had been

careful never to attempt to dominate the movement, he was
considered, as the priest Stephen reported to Christ in his
vision, to be the leader of the Crusade. After his death there was
no one that possessed any over-riding authority. The Count of
Toulouse, who had also long ago discussed Crusading policy
with Pope Urban, inherited his views. But Raymond was not so
able a man, and he could only argue with Bohemond as an
equal, not as the spokesman of the Church. And none of the
princes, in his absence, had sufficient breadth of outlook to see
to the preservation of the unity of Christendom. Adhemar's
charity, his wisdom and his integrity were never questioned by
his comrades, even by those whose ambitions he opposed.
Bohemond's followers mourned his loss as sincerely as did his
own men from France; and Bohemond himself swore to carry
his body to Jerusalem. The whole army was moved and
disquieted by his death.

There was, however, one man that felt no sorrow. Peter
Bartholomew had never forgiven the legate for showing
disbelief in his visions. Two days later he took his revenge. He
announced that he had been visited again by Saint Andrew
who was on this occasion accompanied by Adhemar. Adhemar
announced that, as punishment for his incredulity, he had
spent the intervening hours since his death in hell, from which
he had only been rescued by the prayers of his colleagues and
especially of Bohemond, and by his gift of a few coins for the
upkeep of the Lance. He was forgiven now, and asked that his
body should remain in St Peter's Cathedral at Antioch. Then
Saint Andrew delivered himself of advice to Count Raymond.
Antioch, he said, should be given to its present claimant, if he
were proved to be a righteous man. A Patriarch of the Latin
rite should be elected to decide on his righteousness. The
Crusaders should repent of their sins and march on to
Jerusalem, which was only at ten days' distance; but the
journey would take ten years if they did not return to godlier
habits. That is to say, Peter Bartholomew and his friends
among the Provençals considered that Bohemond should be
allowed to have Antioch, so long as he undertook to help the
Crusade further; that the army should set out soon for

Jerusalem; and that there should be no truck with the Byzantines and the local Orthodox churches.

These revelations were embarrassing to Raymond. He honestly believed in the Holy Lance; and its possession by his troops gave him prestige. For though many might say that the battle against Kerbogha was won by Bohemond's strategy, many others gave the credit of the victory to the relic, and so indirectly to Raymond. But Raymond's other main source of authority sprang from his long association with Adhemar. If the divine messenger who had revealed the position of the Lance were now to question Adhemar's judgement and to repudiate the policy which Raymond had inherited from him and which fitted with Raymond's own views, one or other of Raymond's props must be discarded. He temporized. While remaining loyal to his belief in the Lance, he indicated that he doubted whether Peter Bartholomew's visions continued to be genuine. For, in spite of Saint Andrew's words, he, and others with him, still maintained that Antioch should be given to the Emperor. He found himself in consequence in opposition to most of his troops.

Among the army in general the posthumous attack on Adhemar made a bad impression. Publicizing as it did the legate's disbelief in the relic, it revived the doubt that many had originally felt. In particular, the Normans and the northern French, who had always disliked the Provençals, began to decry the relic and to use the scandal of the forgery to discredit Count Raymond and his plans. In defending Adhemar's reputation they were thus enabled to work against the policy that he had advocated. We may assume that Bohemond enjoyed the situation.

As the epidemic spread through Antioch, the leading Crusaders sought refuge in the country. Bohemond crossed the Amanus mountains into Cilicia, where he strengthened the garrisons left there by Tancred the previous autumn and received their homage. He intended that his principality of Antioch should include the Cilician province. Godfrey went northward, to the towns of Turbessel and Ravendel, which his brother Baldwin handed over to him. Godfrey was jealous of his brother's success; and, as all the princes were seeking territory near Antioch, he wished to have his share. He probably undertook to return the towns to Baldwin, if the army marched on to Palestine. Raymond's movements are uncertain; while Robert of Normandy went to Lattakieh.

Before the Turkish invasions Lattakieh had been the southernmost port of the Byzantine Empire. It had been taken by the Turks about the year 1084 but had later passed under the suzerainty of the Arab Emir of Shaizar. In the autumn of 1097 Guynemer of Boulogne descended upon the port and captured it. His garrison remained in possession over the winter; but in March the fleet commanded by Edgar Atheling, after unloading supplies for the Crusaders at St Symeon, sailed on to Lattakieh. Guynemer's men were driven out and the town taken over in the name of the Emperor. But Edgar could only leave a small detachment to guard the town; so an appeal was made to the Crusading army to supplement the defence. Soon after the victory over Kerbogha Robert of Normandy came in answer to the appeal; and Lattakieh was handed over to him in trust for the Emperor. But Robert's only idea of government was to extract as much money as possible from the governed. So unpopular was his rule that after a few weeks he was forced to retire from the town, which was now given a garrison by the Byzantine governor of Cyprus, Eustathius Philocales.

In September the epidemic abated, and the princes returned to Antioch. On the 11th they met together to draft a letter to Pope Urban to give him the details of the capture of Antioch and to announce the death of his legate. Feeling the need of a supreme authority to overrule the quarrelling factions, they urged him to come in person to the East. Antioch, they pointed out, was a see founded by Saint Peter, and he as Saint Peter's heir should be enthroned there; and he should visit the Holy City itself. They were ready to wait his arrival before marching on into Palestine. Bohemond's name headed the list of princes; and the letter was probably written in his secretariat. The effect of Adhemar's absence was shown by the implied rejection of the rights of the Patriarch John and by a note of hostility towards the native Christian sects, which were denounced as heretical. The Crusaders can hardly have expected that the Pope would be able to journey to the East; but the appeal enabled them to postpone once more the need to decide upon the fate of Antioch; while the Pope would no doubt send a legate who could be given the responsibility for the decision. It was clear by now that the Emperor would not penetrate into Syria this season. Possibly his retreat from Philomelium was already known.

Among the soldiers and pilgrims of the army conditions were very bad. Owing to the fighting no crops had been harvested in the plain of Antioch; and food was still short. Largely to secure supplies Raymond began to organize a raid into Moslem territory. Before he had decided upon his objective he was invited by Godfrey to come on a joint campaign to the town of Azaz, on the main road from Edessa and Turbessel to Antioch. The Emir of Azaz, Omar, was in revolt against his overlord, Ridwan of Aleppo, who was marching to punish him. One of Omar's generals had captured and fallen in love with a Frankish lady, the widow of a Lorrainer knight; and it was on her suggestion that Omar appealed for help to Godfrey. Godfrey responded gladly; for it was inconvenient for him that Azaz should be in Ridwan's hands. Raymond accepted Godfrey's invitation though he insisted that Omar's son should be handed over as a hostage; and Baldwin sent troops from Edessa. At the approach of the Christian army Ridwan retired from Azaz; and Omar was confirmed by Godfrey in its possession, and paid him homage. Raymond was able to collect provisions in the neighbourhood, but suffered heavy losses from Turkish ambushes on the return journey. The episode showed that not only were the Moslem princes prepared now to use Frankish help in their own quarrels, but that the Franks, modifying their militant faith, were prepared to accept Moslem vassals.

In October, in spite of Peter Bartholomew's report that Saint Andrew had again demanded an early departure for Jerusalem, Raymond set out on another raid to secure provisions. He had already occupied Rugia on the Orontes, some thirty miles from

Antioch. From there he attacked the town of Albara, a little to the southeast. The inhabitants, who were all Moslem, capitulated, but were either massacred or sold as slaves in Antioch; and the town was repeopled with Christians. The mosque was converted into a church. To the delight of his army Raymond then appointed one of his priests, Peter of Narbonne, to be its bishop. The appointment was only made because there was no Orthodox bishopric already established in the town. No one yet conceived of a schism between the Greek and Latin churches that would involve a duplication of bishoprics. The new bishop, Latin though he was, was consecrated by the Greek Patriarch, John of Antioch. But Peter of Narbonne's elevation marked the beginning of a Latin church resident in the East, and encouraged those of the Crusaders who, like Peter Bartholomew, were now anxious to see the local Greek ecclesiastics replaced by Latins.

In the debates that followed Kerbogha's defeat, the princes had vowed to start for Jerusalem in November. On 1 November they began to assemble at Antioch to discuss their plans. Raymond came from Albara, where he had left most of his troops. Godfrey rode in from Turbessel, bringing with him the heads of all the Turkish prisoners that he had made in a series of small raids in the district. The Count of Flanders and the Duke of Normandy were already at Antioch; and Bohemond, who had been ill in Cilicia, arrived two days later. On the 5th the princes and their advisers met together in the Cathedral of St Peter. It appeared at once that there was no agreement between them. Bohemond's friends opened by claiming Antioch for him. The Emperor was not coming; and Bohemond was an able man and the Crusader of whom the enemy was most afraid. Raymond retorted by sharply reminding the assembly of the oath to the Emperor that all except himself had sworn. Godfrey and Robert of Flanders were known to favour Bohemond's claim, but dared not speak up for it for fear of the accusation of perjury. The argument continued for several days. Meanwhile the soldiers and pilgrims waiting outside for a declaration grew impatient. Their one desire was to carry out their vows and to reach Jerusalem. They longed to leave

Antioch where they had delayed so long and suffered so much. Spurred on by Peter Bartholomew and his visions, they presented an ultimatum to their chiefs. With an equal contempt for both Bohemond's and Raymond's ambitions, let those, they said, that wished to enjoy the revenues of Antioch do so, and let those that were eager for gifts from the Emperor await his coming; for themselves they would march on to Jerusalem; and if their leaders continued to haggle over the possession of Antioch they would raze its walls before they left. Faced with this and fearing that Raymond and Bohemond would soon resort to arms, the more moderate leaders suggested a more intimate discussion which only the chief princes would attend. There, after further angry scenes, a temporary arrangement was made. Raymond would agree to the decisions that the council might ultimately make about Antioch, so long as Bohemond swore to accompany the Crusade on to Jerusalem; while Bohemond took an oath before the bishops not to delay nor harm the Crusade to suit his personal ambitions. The question of Antioch was not settled; but Bohemond was confirmed in his possession of the citadel and three-quarters of the town, while Raymond remained in control of the fortified bridge and the palace of Yaghi-Siyan, which he placed under William Ermingar. The date for the departure for Jerusalem was still unfixed; but, to occupy the troops meanwhile, it was decided to attack the fortress of Maarat an-Numan, whose reduction was advisable to protect the army's left flank when it should advance southward towards Palestine.

On 23 November Raymond and the Count of Flanders set out for Rugia and Albara and on the 27th they reached the walls of Maarat an-Numan. Their attempted assault on the town next morning was a failure; and when Bohemond and his troops arrived that afternoon and a second assault also failed, it was decided to conduct a regular siege. But, though the town was completely invested, for a fortnight no progress was made. The countryside had to be scoured for wood to make siege machines. Food was short; and detachments of the army would desert their posts in order to search for corn and for vegetables. At last on 11 December, after Peter Bartholomew had announced that success was imminent, a huge wooden castle on wheels, built by Raymond's men and commanded by William of Montpelier, was pushed against one of the city towers. An attempt to scale the tower from it was repulsed; but protection given by the castle enabled the wall on one side of the tower to be mined. In the evening the wall collapsed and a number of humble soldiers forced their way into the town and began to pillage. Meanwhile Bohemond, jealous of Raymond's success and eager to repeat his coup at Antioch, announced by a herald that if the town surrendered to him he would protect the lives of all the defenders that took refuge in a hall near to the main gate. During the night the fighting died down. Many of the citizens, seeing that the defences were pierced, fortified their houses and cisterns but offered to pay a tax if they were spared. Others fled to the hall that Bohemond had indicated. But when the battle reopened next morning no one was spared. The Crusaders poured into the town, massacring everyone that they met and forcing an entrance into the houses, which they looted and burnt. As for the refugees who relied on Bohemond's protection, the men were slaughtered and the women and children sold as slaves.

During the siege Bohemond's and Raymond's troops had cooperated with difficulty. Now, when Bohemond by his treachery had secured the greater part of the loot though it was Raymond's army that had taken the town, the enmity between the southern French and the Normans flared up again. Raymond claimed the town and wished to place it under the Bishop of Albara. But Bohemond would not evacuate his troops unless Raymond abandoned his area of Antioch and, as a counter-attack, he began openly to question the authenticity of visions reported by Peter Bartholomew.

Meanwhile disaffection increased in the whole army. Raymond's troops in particular demanded the resumption of the march on Jerusalem. About Christmas Day representatives of the soldiers indicated to Raymond that if he would organize its departure the army would recognize him as leader of the whole Crusade. Raymond felt that he could not refuse, and a few days later he left Maarat an-Numan for Rugia, announcing that the expedition was about to leave for Palestine. Bohemond thereupon returned to Antioch; and Maarat an-Numan was put into the hands of the Bishop of Albara.

But even after his announcement Raymond delayed. He could not bring himself to leave for the south with Antioch in Bohemond's hands. Bohemond, seeing, perhaps, that the more Raymond hesitated the more mutinous grew his troops, and knowing that the Emperor would not come down across Asia Minor during the winter months, suggested a postponement of the expedition till Easter. To bring matters to a head, Raymond summoned all the princes to meet him at Rugia. There he attempted to buy them to accept his leadership. The sums that he offered presumably corresponded to the strength that each now possessed. To Godfrey he proposed to give ten thousand sous and the same to Robert of Normandy, to Robert of Flanders six thousand, five thousand to Tancred and lesser sums to the lesser chiefs. Bohemond was offered nothing. Raymond hoped that he would thus be established as unquestioned head of the Crusade and could thus keep Bohemond in check. But his overtures were received very coldly.

While the princes conferred at Rugia, the army at Maarat an-Numan took direct action. It was suffering from starvation. All the supplies of the neighbourhood were exhausted; and cannibalism seemed the only solution. Even the Turks were impressed by its tenacity in such conditions, though, as the chronicler Raymond of Aguilers sadly remarks: 'We knew of this too late to profit by it.' The Bishop of Orange, who had some influence over the Provençals, died from these hardships. At last, despite the protests of the Bishop of Albara, the men determined to force Raymond to move by destroying the walls of Maarat an-Numan. At the news, Raymond hurried back to the town but realized that there could be no more postponement.

On 13 January 1099, Raymond and his troops marched out of Maarat an-Numan to continue the Crusade. The count walked barefoot, as befitted the leader of a pilgrimage. To show that there would be no turning back the town was left in flames.

With Raymond were all his vassals. The Bishop of Albara and Raymond Pilet, lord of Tel-Mannas, deserted their towns to travel with him. The garrison that he had kept at Antioch under William Ermingar could not hold out against Bohemond and hastened after him. Of his colleagues among the princes, Robert of Normandy at once set out to join him, accompanied by Tancred, whom Bohemond doubtless wished to watch over Norman-Italian interests in the Crusade. Godfrey of Lorraine and Robert of Flanders hesitated for nearly a month before public opinion forced them to follow. But Baldwin and Bohemond remained in the lands that they had captured.

Thus the quarrel between the two great princes seemed to have found a solution. Raymond was now unchallenged leader of the Crusade; but Bohemond was in possession of Antioch.

The road to Jerusalem

Therefore now go, lead the people unto the place of which
I have spoken unto thee.

Exodus XXXII, 34

When Stephen of Blois, writing to his wife from Nicaea, had
expressed the fear that the Crusade might be held up at
Antioch, he never dreamed how long the delay would last.
Fifteen months had passed since the army had reached the city
walls. During this period there had been important changes in
the Moslem world. The Fatimids of Egypt, like the Byzantines,
had, before the Crusade began, recovered from the first shock
of the Turkish onslaught, and, like the Byzantines, they hoped
to use the Crusade to consolidate their recovery. The real ruler
of Egypt was Shah-an-Shah al-Afdal, who had succeeded his
father, the Armenian renegade Badr al-Jamali, as vizier to the
boy Caliph, al-Mustali. Al-Afdal's embassy to the Crusader
camp at Antioch had not produced any results. Frankish
ambassadors had returned with his envoys to Cairo; but it soon
was clear that they were not authorized to negotiate an alliance
and that the Crusaders, far from being willing to aid the
Egyptians to recover Palestine, had every intention of themselves marching on Jerusalem. Al-Afdal therefore determined
to profit by the war in northern Syria. As soon as he heard of
Kerbogha's defeat at Antioch and realized that the Turks
throughout Asia were in no position to resist a new attack, he
invaded Palestine. The province was still in the hands of the
sons of Ortoq, Soqman and Ilghazi, who admitted the
suzerainty of Duqaq of Damascus. As al-Afdal advanced they

retired behind the walls of Jerusalem. They knew that Duqaq could not at once come to their aid; but they hoped that the great fortifications of Jerusalem and the fighting ability of their Turcoman troops would enable them to hold out till rescue came. Al-Afdal's army was equipped with the latest siege machines, including forty mangonels; but the Ortoqids resisted for forty days, till at last the walls were so battered that they were forced to capitulate. They were allowed to retire with their men to Damascus, whence they joined their cousins in the district round Diarbekir. The Egyptians then occupied the whole of Palestine and by the autumn had fixed their frontier at the pass of the Dog River, on the coast just north of Beirut. In the meantime they repaired the defences of Jerusalem.

In northern Syria the local Arab dynasties were equally delighted by the collapse of Turkish power and were ready to make terms with the Franks. Even the Emir of Hama, Ridwan's father-in-law, and the Emir of Homs, who had fought well for Kerbogha, abandoned any idea of opposing them. More important to the Crusaders was the attitude of the two leading Arab families, the Munqidhites of Shaizar and the Banū 'Ammār of Tripoli. The former controlled the country immediately ahead of the Crusaders, from the Orontes to the coast, and the latter the coast line from the middle Lebanon to the Fatimid frontier. Their friendship, or at least their neutrality, was essential if the Crusade was to advance.

From Maarat an-Numan Raymond marched on to Kafartab, some twelve miles to the south. There he waited till 16 January, collecting provisions to revictual his troops; and there Tancred and Robert of Normandy joined him. Thither, too, came ambassadors from the Emir of Shaizar, offering to provide guides and cheap provisions for the Crusaders if they would pass peaceably through his land. Raymond accepted the offer; and on the 17th the Emir's guides conducted the army across the Orontes, between Shaizar and Hama, and led it up the valley of the Sarout. All the flocks and herds of the district had been driven for safety into a valley adjoining the Sarout; into which, by error, one of the guides introduced the Franks. The herdsmen and the local villagers were not strong enough to prevent the Franks from systematically taking over the beasts. The commander of the castle that dominated the valley thought it best to buy immunity for himself. So rich was the booty that several of the knights went off to sell their surplus in Shaizar and in Hama, in return for packhorses, of which they bought a thousand. The Arab authorities freely allowed them to enter their towns and make their purchases.

While these supplies were being collected, Raymond and his commanders met to discuss what route should now be taken. Raymond himself favoured the view that the army should strike due west across the Nosairi range in order to reach the coast as soon as possible. Lattakieh was already in Christian hands; and so long as he kept to the coast he would be in touch with Antioch and could obtain supplies from the Byzantine authorities in Cyprus, with whom he was on good terms. But Tancred pointed out that to be sure of the coast road it would be necessary to capture all the great fortresses that lay on the way. The fighting strength of the army was now only a thousand knights and five thousand infantrymen. How could such a force indulge in siege warfare? They ought, he argued, to march straight on to Jerusalem, avoiding the necessity of capturing the coastal fortresses. If they could take Jerusalem, not only would the news bring more soldiers out from Europe, but cities like Tripoli, Tyre and Acre could no longer attempt to hold out against them. The argument against his view was that all the country between the Lebanon and the desert was held by Duqaq of Damascus, who, unlike the Arab princelings, would undoubtedly oppose the Crusaders' progress. It was eventually decided to strike the coast further south, through the Buqaia, the plain between the Nosairi range and the Lebanon, which provides the only easy access from inner Syria to the sea, wasting as little time as possible on attempts to reduce enemy fortresses.

On 22 January the Crusaders reached the town of Masyaf whose lord hastened to conclude a treaty with them. From there they turned south-southeast, to avoid the massif of the Jebel Helou. Next day they came to the town of Rafaniya, which they found deserted by its inhabitants but full of supplies of every kind. They remained there for three days, then descended into the Buqaia. The plain was commanded by the huge fortress of Hosn al-Akrad, the Castle of the Kurds, built on the height where the ruins of Krak des Chevaliers now stand. The local inhabitants had driven all their herds to shelter within its walls; and, for the purpose of revictualment rather than for strategic reasons, the Crusaders decided that it must be taken. On 28 January they attacked the fortifications. But the defence, aware of their habits, opened a gate and let out some of their beasts. So intent were the Franks on rounding up all this booty that they scattered; and a sortie from the castle not only prevented them from reassembling but also nearly succeeded in capturing Count Raymond himself, who had been deserted by his bodyguard. Next day the Franks, ashamed of having been tricked, planned a serious assault; but when they reached the walls they found that the castle had been abandoned during the night. There was still considerable booty left within; and the army settled down to spend three weeks there, while further discussions about strategy were held. The Feast of the Purification was celebrated within the castle.

While Raymond was at Hosn al-Akrad, envoys reached him from the Emir of Hama, offering him gifts and promising not to attack his men. They were followed by envoys from the Emir of Tripoli. This Emir, Jalal al-Mulk Abu'l Hasan, of the dynasty of the Banū 'Ammār, a family noted more for its learning than for its warlike qualities, had maintained the independence of his emirate by playing off the Seldjuks against the Fatimids. With the Turkish power in decline, he was ready to encourage the Franks against the renascent Egyptians. Raymond was invited to send representatives to Tripoli to discuss arrangements for the passage of the Crusade and to bring the banners of Toulouse, which the Emir would unfurl over the city. The prosperity of Tripoli and the surrounding country greatly impressed the Frankish ambassadors; who on their return to the camp advised Raymond that if he made a show of force against one of the fortresses of the emirate, the Emir would certainly pay a large sum to buy immunity for the rest of his dominions. Raymond, who was in need of money, took their advice and ordered his army to attack the town of Arqa, situated some fiteen miles from Tripoli, where the Buqaia opens out to the coast. He arrived before its walls on 14 February.

Meanwhile, anxious as he was to establish communications with the garrison at Lattakieh and the sea, Raymond encouraged Raymond Pilet and Raymond, Viscount of Turenne, to attempt a surprise attack on Tortosa, the one good harbour on the coast between Lattakieh and Tripoli. The two Raymonds, with a small detachment, hurried westward and arrived before the town after dark on 16 February. They lit a series of camp fires all round the walls, to suggest the presence of a far larger army than they possessed. The ruse was successful. The governor of Tortosa, who was subject to the Emir of Tripoli, was so seriously alarmed that he evacuated himself and his garrison by sea during the night. Next morning the gates of the town were opened to the Franks. At the news of their conquest the governor of Marqiye, ten miles to the north, hastened to recognize Raymond's suzerainty. The capture of Tortosa greatly strengthened the Crusade. It opened up easy communications by sea with Antioch and Cyprus and with Europe.

This success roused jealousy among the Crusaders still at Antioch and decided them to follow Raymond southward. About the end of February Godfrey of Lorraine, Bohemond and Robert of Flanders set out from Antioch to Lattakieh. There Bohemond turned back. He thought that after all it would be wiser to consolidate himself in Antioch lest the Emperor might march towards Syria in the spring. Godfrey and Robert moved on to besiege the small sea-port of Jabala. While they lay there, the Bishop of Albara reached them from Raymond, begging them to join him at Arqa.

The siege of Arqa was not going well. The town was well fortified and courageously defended; and Raymond's army was not large enough to invest it completely. Tancred's warning that the army was in no condition to attempt to storm fortresses was fully justified. But once Raymond had begun the siege he could not abandon it for fear that the Emir of Tripoli, seeing his weakness, would become openly hostile. It is possible that the soldiers made no great effort. Life was comfortable in the camp. The countryside was fertile and further supplies began to arrive through Tortosa. After all that they had endured the men were pleased to relax themselves a while. Early in March there was a rumour that a Moslem army was assembling to relieve Arqa, led in person by the Caliph of Baghdad. The rumour was false, but it alarmed Raymond into summoning Godfrey and Robert of Flanders. On the receipt of the message Godfrey and Robert made a truce with the Emir of Jabala, who accepted their suzerainty, and hurried southward to Arqa. They celebrated their arrival by an attack on the suburbs of Tripoli and by several successful raids to round up beasts of all sorts, including camels, in the Buqaia.

Raymond soon regretted the arrival of his colleagues. He had been for two months the accepted leader of the Crusade. Even Tancred had acknowledged his authority in return for five thousand sous. But now he had been obliged to call on his rivals for help. Tancred, whose advice he had ignored, moved over to Godfrey's camp, saying that Raymond had not paid him sufficiently. The two Roberts showed little inclination to admit Raymond's hegemony. In his attempt to assert his rights he aroused resentment; and quarrels began. The men of each army, seeing their leaders at loggerheads, followed suit and would not cooperate with each other.

The controversy was worsened by the arrival in early April of letters from the Emperor. Alexius informed the Crusaders that he was now ready to start out for Syria. If they would wait for him till the end of June, he would be with them by St John's Day and would lead them on into Palestine. Raymond wished to accept the offer. As the Emperor's faithful ally he could count on imperial backing to help him to reassert his supremacy over the Frankish army. Amongst his own men, there were many, like Raymond of Aguilers, who, much as they disliked the Byzantines, felt that the Emperor's arrival would at least provide the Crusade with a leader whom all the princes would admit. But the bulk of the army was impatient to move on to Jerusalem; and none of the other princes wished to find himself under imperial suzerainty. Against such strong public opinion, Raymond's policy could not prevail. It is probable that Alexius never expected that the Crusaders would wait for him. Disgusted by their behaviour at Antioch he had already decided upon an attitude of neutrality. This to a Byzantine diplomat was not a passive attitude but meant the establishment of relations with both sides in order that benefits might be reaped whichever should be victorious. He was in communication with the Egyptians, who had probably written to him when the Crusade advanced towards their territory to ask if it was acting on his account. In answer Alexius repudiated the movement. He had reason for so doing. Bohemond's actions taught him that he could not count upon the loyalty of the Franks; nor was he particularly interested in Palestine. It lay outside the lands that he had hoped to recover for the Empire. His only obligation there was towards the Orthodox Christians, whose protector he was. He may well have considered that they would fare better under the tolerant rule of the Fatimids than under the Franks who were already showing at Antioch a marked hostility towards native Christianity. At the same time he did not wish to sever his connection with the Crusade, which might still be of use to the Empire. His correspondence with Egypt later fell into the hands of the Crusaders, who were genuinely shocked by the evidence of his treachery to them, though their treachery to him seemed to them perfectly reasonable and right. They blamed it on him that the ambassadors they had sent to Cairo from Antioch had been detained there for so long.

These ambassadors returned to the army at Arqa a few days later, bearing the Fatimids' final offer for a settlement. If the Crusade would abandon any attempt to force its way into Fatimid territory, its pilgrims would be allowed free access to the holy places and everything would be done to facilitate the pilgrimage. The suggestion was at once rejected.

In spite of the desire of the other princes to resume the march, Raymond refused to leave Arqa untaken. To bring matters to a head, Peter Bartholomew announced that on 5 April Christ, Saint Peter and Saint Andrew had all appeared to him to announce that an immediate assault on Arqa must be made. The bulk of the army was growing tired of Peter's revelations, which they regarded as a political device of Count Raymond's. A section of the northern French, led by Robert of Normandy's chaplain, Arnulf of Rohes, now openly declared their disbelief and even questioned the authenticity of the Holy Lance, remarking that Adhemar of Le Puy had never been convinced of it. The Provençals rallied to Peter's support. Stephen of Valence reminded the army of his vision at Antioch. Raymond of Aguilers told how he had kissed the Lance while it was still embedded in the ground. Another priest, Peter Desiderius, reported that Adhemar had appeared to him after his death and had described the hell-fire to which his doubts had led him. Another, Everard, said that when he was visiting Tripoli on business during the Turkish siege of Antioch a Syrian there had told him of a vision in which Saint Mark had spoken of the Lance. The Bishop of Apt, who had been a sceptic, mentioned a vision that had caused him to change his mind. One of Adhemar's own entourage, Bertrand of Le Puy, announced that the bishop and his standard-bearer had both come to him in a vision to admit that the Lance was genuine. Faced by this impressive evidence, Arnulf publicly confessed that he was convinced; but his friends continued to cast doubt on the whole story; till at last Peter Bartholomew in a fury demanded to be allowed to defend himself by the ordeal of fire. Whatever the truth may have been, he clearly by now believed firmly in his divine inspiration.

The ordeal took place on Good Friday, 8 April. Two piles of logs, blessed by the bishops, were erected in a narrow passage and set alight. Peter Bartholomew, clad only in a tunic, with the Lance in his hand, leapt quickly through the flames. He emerged horribly burnt and would have collapsed back into the fire had not Raymond Pilet caught hold of him. For twelve days he lingered on in agony, then died of his wounds. As a result of the ordeal the Lance was utterly discredited, save only by the Provençals, who maintained that Peter had passed safely through the flames but had been pushed back by the enthusiastic crowd in their eagerness to touch his sacred tunic.

Count Raymond still kept the Lance with all reverence in his chapel.

The army lingered on for a month outside Arqa before Raymond could be induced to abandon the siege. The fighting there had cost many lives, including that of Anselm of Ribemont, whose letters to his liege lord, the Archbishop of Reims, had given a vivid account of the Crusade. On 13 May Raymond yielded to his colleagues' persuasion and, with tears in his eyes, ordered the camp to be struck; and the whole host moved down to Tripoli. There had been further discussions about the route to be followed. The Syrians informed Raymond that there was an easy road passing through Damascus, but though food was plentiful there, water was short. The road over the Lebanon was well watered, but it was difficult for beasts of burden. The third alternative was the coast road; but there were many places where it could be blocked by a handful of the enemy. However, local prophecies declared that the deliverers of Jerusalem would travel along the coast. This was the road that was chosen, less for its prophetic reputation than for the contact that it provided with the English and Genoese fleets that were now cruising in Levantine waters.

As the Crusaders approached, the Emir of Tripoli hastened to buy immunity for his capital and its suburbs by releasing some three hundred Christian captives that were in the town. He compensated them with fifteen thousand bezants and fifteen fine horses; and he provided pack-animals and provender for the whole army. He was further reported to have offered to embrace Christianity if the Franks defeated the Fatimids.

On Monday, 16 May, the Crusaders left Tripoli, accompanied by guides provided by the Emir; who led them safely along the dangerous road that rounded the cape of Ras Shaqqa. Passing peacefully through the Emir's towns of Batrun and Jebail, they reached the Fatimid frontier on the Dog River on 19 May. The Fatimids kept no troops in their northern territory, except for small garrisons in the towns on the coast, but they possessed a considerable navy, which could provide additional defence for these towns. Thus, though the Crusaders did not meet with any opposition on the road, they could not hope to capture any of the ports that they passed; and the Christian fleet could no longer keep in touch with them. Fear of running short of supplies obliged them thenceforward to hurry on as quickly as possible to their final objective.

As they drew near to Beirut the local inhabitants, dreading the destruction of the rich gardens and orchards that surrounded the city, hastened to offer them gifts and a free passage through their lands on condition that the fruit trees, the vines and the crops were unharmed. The princes accepted the terms and led the army quickly on to Sidon, which was reached on 20 May. The garrison of Sidon was of sterner stuff and made a sortie against the Crusaders as they were encamped on the banks of the Nahr al-Awali. The sortie was repulsed; and the Crusaders retorted by ravaging the gardens in the suburbs. But they moved on as soon as possible to the neighbourhood of Tyre, where they waited two days to allow Baldwin of Le Bourg and a number of knights from Antioch and from Edessa to catch them up. The streams and greenery of the neighbourhood made it a delightful halting-place. The garrison of Tyre stayed behind its walls and did not molest them. Tyre was left on the 23rd; and the army crossed without difficulty over the pass called the Ladder of Tyre and over the heights of Naqoura, and arrived outside Acre on the 24th. The governor, following the example of Beirut, secured immunity for the fertile farms around the town by the gift of ample provisions. From Acre the army marched to Haifa and along the coast under Mount Carmel to Caesarea, where four days were spent, from the 26th to the 30th, in order that Whitsun might be properly celebrated. While it was encamped there a pigeon was killed by a hawk overhead and fell near the tent of the Bishop of Apt. It was found to be a carrier, with a message from the governor of Acre to rouse the Moslems of Palestine against the invaders.

When the march was resumed, the coast was followed only as far as Arsuf, where the army turned inland, arriving before Ramleh on 3 June. Ramleh, unlike most of the towns of Palestine, was a Moslem town. Before the Turkish invasions it had been the administrative capital of the province, but had declined in recent years. The approach of the Crusaders alarmed the inhabitants; the garrison was small and they were too far from the sea for the Egyptian navy to help them. They fled in a body from their homes, away toward the southwest, having first, as an act of defiance, destroyed the great Church of St George that stood in the ruined village of Lydda, a mile from Ramleh. When Robert of Flanders and Gaston of Béarn rode up in the van of the Crusading army they found the streets deserted and the houses empty.

The occupation of a Moslem town in the heart of the Holy Land elated the Crusaders. They vowed at once to rebuild the sanctuary of St George and to erect Ramleh and Lydda into a lordship to be his patrimony, and to create a new diocese whose bishop should be its lord. A Norman priest, Robert of Rouen, was appointed to the see. As at Albara this did not mean the displacement of a Greek bishop in favour of a Latin, but the establishment of a bishopric in conquered Moslem country. The appointment showed that public opinion amongst the Crusaders considered that conquered territory should be given to the Church. Robert was left in charge of Ramleh with a small garrison to protect him. Meanwhile the princes debated what next should be done; for some considered that it would be foolish to attack Jerusalem in the height of summer. It would be better, they argued, to advance against the real enemy, Egypt. After some discussion their advice was rejected and the march to Jerusalem was resumed on 6 June.

From Ramleh the army took the old road that winds up into the Judaean hills to the north of the present thoroughfare. As it passed through the village of Emmaus envoys came to the princes from the city of Bethlehem, whose entirely Christian population begged to be delivered from the yoke of the Moslems. Tancred and Baldwin of Le Bourg at once rode off with a small detachment of knights over the hills to Bethlehem. They arrived in the middle of the night, and the frightened citizens at first believed them to be part of an Egyptian army come to reinforce the defence of Jerusalem. When dawn broke and the knights were recognized as Christians, the whole city came out in procession, with all the relics and the crosses from the Church of the Nativity, to welcome their rescuers and to kiss their hands.

While the birthplace of Christ was being restored to Christian rule, the main Christian army pressed on all day and through the night towards Jerusalem. It was heartened by an eclipse of the moon, foreboding the eclipse of the Crescent. Next morning a hundred of Tancred's knights from Bethlehem rejoined their comrades. Later in the morning, the Crusaders reached the summit of the road, at the Mosque of the prophet Samuel, on the hilltop that the pilgrims called Montjoie; and Jerusalem with its walls and towers rose in the distance before them. By that evening of Tuesday, 7 June 1099, the Christian army was encamped before the Holy City.

CHAPTER 14

The triumph of the Cross

Shout unto God with the voice of triumph. For the Lord
most high is terrible.

Psalms XLVII, 1, 2

The city of Jerusalem was one of the great fortresses of the
medieval world. Since the days of the Jebusites its site had been
famed for its strength, which the skill of men had improved
down the centuries. The walls beneath which the Crusaders
found themselves followed the same line as the walls built later
by the Ottoman Sultan, Suleiman the Magnificent, which
surround the old city today. They had been laid out when
Hadrian rebuilt the city; and the Byzantines, the Ommayads
and the Fatimids in turn had added to them and repaired
them. On the east the wall was protected by the steep slopes of
the ravine of the Kedron. On the southeast the ground fell to
the Vale of Gehenna. A third valley that was only slightly less
deep skirted the western wall. It was only on the southwest,
where the wall cut across Mount Sion, and along the length of
the northern wall that the terrain favoured an attack on the
fortifications. The citadel, the Tower of David, was placed
halfway down the western wall, commanding the road that
slanted up the hillside to the Jaffa Gate. Though there were no
springs within the city, its ample cisterns secured the water
supply. The Roman drainage system, still in use in the
twentieth century, kept it from disease.

The defence of the city was in the hands of the Fatimid
governor, Iftikhar ad-Daula. The walls were in good condition;
and he had a strong garrison of Arab and Sudanese troops. On

the news of the Franks' approach he took the precaution of blocking or poisoning the wells outside the city, and driving the flocks and herds from the pastures round the city into places of safety. Next, he ordered all the Christian population of the city, Orthodox and heretic alike, to retire outside the city walls. The Jews, however, were permitted to remain within. It was a wise move. In the tenth century the Christians outnumbered the Moslems in Jerusalem; and though the Caliph Hakim's persecutions had reduced their numbers, and though many more, including most of the Orthodox clergy, had departed with the Patriarch during the uneasy times that followed Ortoq's death, there were still thousands left, useless as fighting men as they were forbidden to carry arms, and unreliable in a battle against fellow Christians. Moreover their exile meant that there would be fewer mouths to feed in the beleaguered city. At the same time Iftikhar sent urgently to Egypt for armed aid.

Even had the lie of the land permitted it, the Crusaders had insufficient forces to invest the whole city. They concentrated their strength on the sectors where they could come near to the walls. Robert of Normandy took up his station along the northern wall opposite to the Gate of Flowers (Herod's Gate), with Robert of Flanders on his right, opposite to the Gate of the Column (St Stephen's or the Damascus Gate). Godfrey of Lorraine took over the area covering the northwest angle of the city, as far down as the Jaffa Gate. He was joined here by Tancred, who rode up when the army was already in position, bringing flocks that he had taken on his way from Bethlehem. To his south was Raymond of Toulouse, who, finding that the valley kept him too far from the walls, moved up after two or three days on to Mount Sion. The eastern and southeastern sectors were left unguarded.

The siege began on 7 June, the very day that the Crusade arrived at the walls. But it was soon clear that time was on the side of the besieged. Iftikhar was well supplied with food and water. His armaments were better than the Franks'; and he was able to strengthen his towers with sacks full of cotton and of hay, which enabled them to withstand the shock of the bombardment by the Frankish mangonels. If he could hold out till the relieving army from Egypt appeared, all would be over with the Crusade. But, large though the garrison was, it was barely sufficient to man all the walls. The Crusaders on their part soon were in difficulties over their water supply. Iftikhar's measures had been effective. The only source of pure water available to the besiegers came from the pool of Siloam, below the south walls, which was dangerously exposed to missiles from the city. To supplement their supplies of water, they had to travel six miles or more. Knowing this, the garrison would send out small companies to ambush the paths to the springs. Many soldiers and pilgrims perished from such surprise attacks. Food also began to run short; for little could be obtained near the city. Heat and dust and lack of shade added to the discomfort of the Crusaders, coming as they did from cooler climates and wearing, many of them, armour ill-suited to the Judaean summer. It was clear to them all that they could not afford a long siege but must quickly take the city by assault.

On 12 June the princes made a pilgrimage to the Mount of Olives. There an aged hermit addressed them, bidding them attack the walls on the morrow. They protested that they lacked the machines for a successful assault; but the hermit would have none of that. If they had faith, God. he said, would give them the victory. Emboldened by his words, they ordered a general attack to be made next morning. But the hermit was mistaken or else their faith was too weak. The Crusaders went to the attack with great fervour and soon overran the outer defences of the north wall. But they had too few ladders to be able to scale the walls simultaneously in a sufficient number of places. After several hours of desperate fighting they saw that their attempts were useless and withdrew.

The failure of the assault caused bitter disappointment; but it made clear to the princes the need for building more siege machines. At a council on 15 June they decided to withhold further attacks till they were better supplied with mangonels and ladders. But they lacked the material with which to build them. As at Antioch, they were now saved by the timely arrival of help from the sea. On 17 June six Christian vessels put into

the harbour of Jaffa, which they found deserted by the
Moslems. The squadron consisted of two Genoese galleys,
under the brothers Embriaco, and four ships probably from the
English fleet. They were carrying food supplies and armaments,
including the ropes, nails and bolts required for making siege
machines. Hearing of their arrival the Crusaders at once sent a
small detachment to establish contact with them. Near Ramleh
these troops were ambushed by a Moslem company, operating
from Ascalon, and were only rescued by the coming of
Raymond Pilet and his men close on their heels. Meanwhile an
Egyptian fleet appeared off the coast and blockaded Jaffa. One
of the English ships slipped through the blockade and sailed
back to Lattakieh. The other ships were abandoned by their
crews as soon as the cargo was landed; and the sailors marched
up under Raymond Pilet's escort to the camp outside
Jerusalem. They themselves and the goods that they brought
were very welcome. But it was still necessary to find wood with
which to build the machines. Little was to be obtained on the
bare hills round Jerusalem; and the Crusaders were obliged to
send expeditions for many miles to collect what was required.
It was only when Tancred and Robert of Flanders penetrated
with their followers as far as the forests round Samaria and
came back laden with logs and planks carried on camel-back or
by captive Moslems, that work could start upon the machines.
Scaling ladders were made; and Raymond and Godfrey each
began to construct a wooden castle fitted with catapults and set
on wheels. Gaston of Béarn was responsible for the construction
of Godfrey's castle, and William Ricou of Raymond's.

But the work went slowly; and meanwhile the Franks
suffered terribly from the heat. For many days the sirocco blew,
with its deadly effect on the nerves of men unused to it. The
provision of water grew increasingly difficult. Numbers of the
pack-animals and the herds that the army had collected died
daily from thirst. Detachments would go as far as the Jordan to
find water. The native Christians were well-disposed and acted
as guides to the springs and the forests of the neighbourhood;
but it was impossible to prevent forays and ambushes from
Moslem soldiers, either of the garrison or of companies that

were wandering freely round the country. Quarrels arose again among the princes, concerning, first, the possession of Bethlehem. Tancred had liberated the town and had left his banner waving over the Church of the Nativity. But the clergy and the rival princes felt it to be wrong that so holy a building should be in the power of one secular lord. Tancred defended his claims to Bethlehem; and, though public opinion was against him, the matter was deferred. Next, discussions were begun about the future status of Jerusalem. Some of the knights suggested that a king should be appointed; but the clergy unanimously opposed this, saying that no Christian could call himself king in the city where Christ was crowned and suffered. Here again public opinion was on the side of the clergy; and further discussions were postponed. Their physical miseries, combined with disappointment at the failure of the attempted assault and the renewed quarrels of the princes, induced many of the Crusaders even now to desert the Crusade. A company of them went down to the Jordan to undergo rebaptism in the holy river; then, after gathering palm branches from the river bank, they journeyed straight down to Jaffa, hoping to find boats to carry them back to Europe.

Early in July it was learnt in the camp that a great army had set out from Egypt to relieve Jerusalem. The princes realized that there was no time for delay. But the morale of their men was low. Once more a vision came to their support. On the morning of 6 July the priest Peter Desiderius, who had already testified that he had seen Bishop Adhemar after his death, came to Adhemar's brother, William-Hugh of Monteil, and to his lord, Isoard of Gap, to say that the bishop had again appeared to him. After ordering the Crusaders to give up their selfish schemes, Adhemar ordered them to hold a fast and to walk in procession barefoot round the walls of Jerusalem. If they did so with repentant hearts, within nine days they would capture Jerusalem. When Peter Desiderius had claimed to see Adhemar suffering hell-fire for his doubting of the Holy Lance, he had been widely disbelieved; but now, perhaps because the beloved bishop was shown in a nobler light, and because the family of Monteil gave their support, the vision was at once accepted as

genuine by all the army. Adhemar's instructions were eagerly
obeyed. A fast was commanded and steadfastly observed
during the next three days. On Friday, 8 July, a solemn
procession wound round the path that surrounded the city.
The bishops and priests of the Crusade came first, bearing
crosses and their holy relics. The princes and the knights
followed, then the foot soldiers and the pilgrims. All were
barefoot. The Moslems gathered on the walls to mock them;
but they gloried in such mockery, and having completed the
circuit ascended the Mount of Olives. There Peter the Hermit
preached to them and after him Raymond's chaplain,
Raymond of Aguilers, and Robert of Normandy's chaplain,
Arnulf of Rohes, who was now considered the finest preacher
with the army. Their eloquence moved and excited the host.
Even Raymond and Tancred forgot their quarrels and vowed
to fight together for the Cross.

The enthusiasm lasted on. During the next two days, in spite
of their sufferings from thirst, the men of the army worked hard
to complete the great siege towers. The skill of the Genoese,
under William Embriaco, was of great assistance; and even the
old men and the women did their part in sewing ox-hide and
camel-hide and nailing it on the exposed parts of the woodwork,
as a protection against the Greek fire used by the Saracens. On
the 10th the wooden structures were ready and were wheeled
up to their stations, the one against the north wall and the other
on Mount Sion. A third, slightly smaller, was built to go against
the northwest corner of the defences. The work of construction
had been carefully carried on out of sight of the soldiers of the
garrison; who were astounded and alarmed to find such castles
opposing them. The governor, Iftikhar, hastened to reinforce
the weaker sections of the defences; and the siege towers were
steadily bombarded with stones and with liquid fire to prevent
them from closing in against the walls.

It was decided that the assault should begin during the night
of 13–14 July. The main attack would be launched simultaneously from Mount Sion and on the eastern sector of the
northern wall, with a feint attack on the northwest angle.
According to Raymond of Aguilers, whose figures need not be

doubted, the effective fighting strength of the army was now twelve thousand foot-soldiers and twelve or thirteen hundred knights. There were in addition many pilgrims, whose numbers he does not try to assess, men too old or too sick to fight, and women and children. The first task of the assailants was to bring their wooden castles right up to the walls; which involved the filling up of the ditch that ran round their feet. All night long and during the day of the 14th the Crusaders concentrated on their task, suffering heavily from the stones and the liquid fire of the defence, and answering with a heavy bombardment from their own mangonels. By the evening of the 14th Raymond's men had succeeded in wheeling their tower over the ditch against the wall. But the defence was fierce; for it seems that Iftikhar himself commanded in this sector. Raymond could not establish a foothold on the wall itself. Next morning Godfrey's tower closed in on the north wall, close to the present Gate of Flowers. Godfrey and his brother, Eustace of Boulogne, commanded from the upper storey. About midday they succeeded in making a bridge from the tower to the top of the wall; and two Flemish knights, Litold and Gilbert of Tournai, led the pick of the Lotharingian army across, followed soon by Godfrey himself. Once a sector of the wall was captured, scaling ladders enabled many more of the assailants to climb into the city. While Godfrey remained on the wall encouraging the newcomers and sending men to open the Gate of the Column to the main forces of the Crusade, Tancred and his men, who had been close behind the Lorrainers, penetrated deep into the city streets. The Moslems, seeing their defences broken, fled towards the Haram es-Sherif, the Temple area, where the Dome of the Rock and the Mosque of al-Aqsa stood, intending to use the latter as their last fortress. But they had no time to put it into a state of defence. As they crowded in and up on the roof, Tancred was upon them. Hastily they surrendered to him, promising a heavy ransom, and took his banner to display it over the mosque. He had already desecrated and pillaged the Dome of the Rock. Meanwhile the inhabitants of the city fled back in confusion towards the southern quarters, where Iftikhar was still holding out against Raymond. Early in the afternoon

he realized that all was lost. He withdrew into the Tower of
David, which he offered to hand over to Raymond with a great
sum of treasure in return for his life and the lives of his
bodyguard. Raymond accepted the terms and occupied the
Tower. Iftikhar and his men were safely escorted out of the city
and permitted to join the Moslem garrison of Ascalon.

They were the only Moslems in Jerusalem to save their lives.
The Crusaders, maddened by so great a victory after such
suffering, rushed through the streets and into the houses and
mosques killing all that they met, men, women and children
alike. All that afternoon and all through the night the massacre
continued. Tancred's banner was no protection to the refugees
in the Mosque of al-Aqsa. Early next morning a band of
Crusaders forced an entry into the mosque and slew everyone.
When Raymond of Aguilers later that morning went to visit the
Temple area he had to pick his way through corpses and blood
that reached up to his knees.

The Jews of Jerusalem fled in a body to their chief synagogue.
But they were held to have aided the Moslems; and no mercy
was shown to them. The building was set on fire and they were
all burnt within.

The massacre at Jerusalem profoundly impressed all the
world. No one can say how many victims it involved; but it
emptied Jerusalem of its Moslem and Jewish inhabitants.
Many even of the Christians were horrified by what had been
done; and amongst the Moslems, who had been ready hitherto
to accept the Franks as another factor in the tangled politics of
the time, there was henceforward a clear determination that
the Franks must be driven out. It was this bloodthirsty proof of
Christian fanaticism that recreated the fanaticism of Islam.
When, later, wiser Latins in the East sought to find some basis
on which Christian and Moslem could work together, the
memory of the massacre stood always in their way.

When there were no more Moslems left to be slain, the
princes of the Crusade went in solemn state through the
desolate Christian quarter, deserted since Iftikhar had exiled its
inhabitants, to give thanks to God in the Church of the Holy
Sepulchre. Then, on 17 July, they met together to appoint a
ruler for the conquered city.

The ruler whom most would have welcomed was dead. The whole army grieved that Bishop Adhemar of Le Puy should not be living to see the triumph of the cause that he had served. It was not to be believed that he had not really seen it. Soldier after soldier testified that there had been a warrior fighting in the forefront of the assault, in whom they had recognized the features of the Bishop. Others too, who would have rejoiced in the victory, did not survive to hear of it. Symeon, Patriarch of Jerusalem, had died a few days earlier in exile in Cyprus. Far away in Italy the founder of the Crusade was lying sick. On 29 July 1099, a fortnight after his soldiers had entered the Holy City, but before any news of it could reach him, Pope Urban II died at Rome.

Epilogue

With the recovery of Jerusalem for Christendom the First Crusade reached its triumphant climax. But there was still much to be done if the Holy Land was to remain in Christian hands. During the next three years three great Egyptian armies had to be driven back. It was not till 1124 that the occupation of Palestine and maritime Syria was completed by the capture of Tyre.

By that time all the great leaders of the First Crusade were dead. With the capture of Jerusalem it had been necessary to find a ruler for the Christian dominion that was to be founded. Pope Urban had envisaged a theocratic state; and, had his legate Adhemar been still alive, he would doubtless have been accepted as its regent. But there was now no Papal legate with the army. A lay ruler seemed desirable. Of the princes present at the capture of Jerusalem the Count of Flanders and the Duke of Normandy, both greatly respected, were anxious to return home, as was Godfrey of Lorraine's elder brother, Eustace of Boulogne, a man with little ambition. The Norman Tancred was regarded as Bohemond's poor relation; and Bohemond was reigning at Antioch. This left Raymond of Toulouse and Godfrey of Lorraine. An electoral body composed of the leading clerics and knights offered the throne of Jerusalem to Raymond. He was the richest of the princes, with the largest army, and he had been the personal friend of Pope Urban and of Adhemar. He refused the offer, saying that he could not bear the title of king in a city that was Christ's. The pious sentiment may have been genuine; but he realized, too, that he was not popular with the army in general and that many of his own troops were eager to go home. However, he was not pleased when the electors then approached Godfrey, who accepted the royal power but took the modest title of *Advocatus Sancti Sepulchri*, or dedicated defender of the Holy Sepulchre. Raymond retired for a while to Constantinople but returned two years later to carve for himself and his descendants a County out of the rich lands of the Lebanon based on Tripoli. He died in 1105, before the task was fully completed.

Godfrey lived on for a year, successful in warfare but incompetent as an administrator. On his death in July 1100, his brother Baldwin came from Edessa, leaving the County to his cousin, Baldwin of Rethel, and took over Jerusalem, with the title of King. Under his able government the Kingdom of Jerusalem was well established. He died in 1118. In that same year the Emperor Alexius died in Constantinople.

Of the other great princes, Bohemond was Prince of Antioch. He made a pilgrimage to Jerusalem at the end of 1099. He had hopes of taking over its government when Godfrey should die. But in August 1100, before he had heard of Godfrey's death, he had led a rash expedition against the Turks and had been captured by the Danishmend emir. On his release from captivity nearly two years later, he found his nephew Tancred established in Antioch. He decided to return, at least temporarily, to his lands in southern Italy. After visiting Rome and the Court of France he recruited a new Crusading force which was to begin its campaign with a war against the Emperor Alexius. Late in 1107 he crossed the Adriatic to besiege Dyrrhachium. But he did not have command of the sea; and the Imperial army was now a formidable force. It surrounded Bohemond's troops and then waited till disease and lack of supplies forced them to surrender. Bohemond never recovered from the humiliation. He returned to Italy and died there in 1111, an obscure Apulian princeling. However, on Tancred's death, Bohemond's son succeeded to Antioch.

Robert of Flanders, Robert of Normandy and Eustace of Boulogne all returned safely to their lands. In 1118, when news came to Europe of the death of Baldwin of Jerusalem, Eustace, as his brother, felt that he ought to go out to claim the inheritance. But when he reached Apulia he learnt that the throne had gone to his cousin, Baldwin of Rethel, Count of Edessa. He returned to Boulogne, it seems with a sigh of relief.

Stephen of Blois, who had shamefully fled from the Crusade when it lay before Antioch, was ordered by his angry wife to return to the East in 1101. A year later, to her satisfaction, he died a hero's death in battle against the Egyptians.

The Crusading movement was to end in tragedy. Within two centuries the last Crusader settlement on the Asian mainland had fallen back into the hands of the Moslems, Moslems more hostile and bitter than any had been before the Holy War. The extraordinary success of the First Crusade had been largely due to the help given by Byzantium and, still more, to the disunity of the Moslem world. When Byzantium was to collapse, owing chiefly to the ungrateful enmity of the Crusaders themselves, and when the Moslem world was to find leaders such as Saladin, the Crusader states in Palestine and Syria were doomed. But all that lay hidden in the future. To the men and women of the time the triumph of the First Crusade was a miracle. It justified the cries that greeted the great Pope when he preached the Holy War at Clermont, the cries of 'Deus le volt.' It had been the will of God.

Index